Investing with a Computer

A Time-series Analysis Approach

Investing with a Computer

A Time-series Analysis Approach

Herb Brooks

PBI
a petrocelli book
new york / princeton

Designed by Diane L. Backes
Typesetting by Backes Graphics

Printed in the United States of America
1 2 3 4 5 6 7 8 9 10

Library of Congress Cataloging in Publication Data

Brooks, Herb.
Investing with a computer.

Bibliography: p.
Includes index.
1. Investments – Data processing. 2. Stock price forecasting – Data processing. I. Title.
HG4515.5.B76 1984 332.6'028'5425 83-19395
ISBN 0-89433-194-9

To
Betty, Virginia and Steve

CONTENTS

PREFACE

This book shows how you can use your computer to analyze stock price movements. Chapter 2 discusses the detection of a new trend, and Chapters 3 through 7 discuss filtering and the detection of oscillations, which can be useful for prediction. Chapters 8 through 10 are intended for the serious worker; however, it is suggested that the reader will benefit from reading straight through the book the first time, without stopping to puzzle out everything. Then he can return to study what is of most interest.

I wish to acknowledge the help of Henry Alken, who performed the filtering of the business cycle (Chapter 7). Also portions of this material were published previously in *Cycles Magazine* and in *The MicroComputer Investor.* I am indebted to

Gertrude Shirk, Editor
Foundation for the Study of Cycles
124 S. Highland Ave.
Pittsburgh, PA 15206
(copyright 1972, 1973, 1980)

and to

Jack M. Williams, Administrator
MicroComputer Investors Association
902 Anderson Drive
Fredericksburg, VA 22405
(copyright 1978, 1980, 1981)

for their kind permissions to reprint.

1
Introduction

Experience is a good school, but the fees are high.
HEINRICH HEINE

Your home computer can help you study and understand the stock market.

People who buy and sell stocks are interested in price *movement*. Even if you only buy stocks to hold for long-term investment, you will be better off to buy when prices are low. Also, bond prices vary with the cycle in interest rates.

I think most people should invest, and I think everyone should study business cycles to make the most of his or her investments and career. And the ideal tool for understanding market cycles is a computer.

A computer can help you to detect the onset of a major bullish move in a stock such as Xerox (Figure 1-1). However, we do not need such a stock to make money. A fluctuation can also be profitable if we know the timing of its up and down movements so that we buy and sell at the right times. Many of the movements in stock prices are not predictable, and that means we will lose part of the time. What we are going to look for are fluctuations that *are* predictable, that is, *regular oscillations.* With a regular oscillation that is large enough, we can win more times than we lose.

There are regular oscillations in the optimism of the market. These are most clearly seen in an average of stock

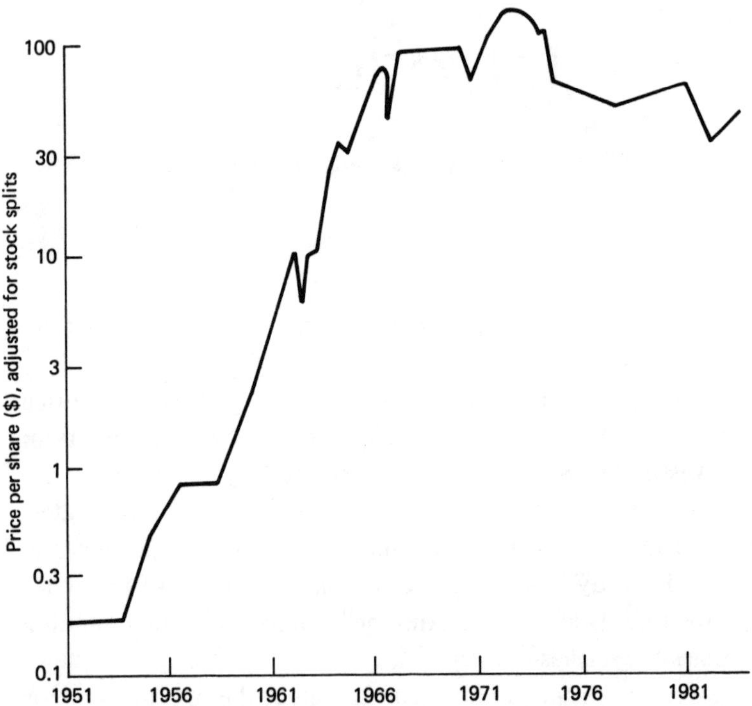

FIGURE 1-1. The smashing success of Xerox.

prices known as an index. (Most of the charts in this book are based on the Dow Jones Industrial Index.) To take advantage of these market oscillations, you can invest in the stock of your choice; or you can invest in a mutual fund, which also averages the prices of many stocks; or if you really want to speculate, you can buy an option on a stock price index.

How about the other half of the cycle, when prices go down ("bear" markets)? You might be able to profit in bear markets by "selling short"; when prices go down, you can cover your short position by "buying in" at a profit. However, selling short is rarely advisable. The reasons for this are given later, in Chapter 10.

A way to detect these trends, and a way to study regular oscillations, is with filters. This book is mostly about filters and how to use them in your computer.

Filters were developed by astronomers and statisticians, and later by communications engineers. They are a mathematical tool, but your computer does the mathematics. The way in which the filters perform their functions can be understood without higher mathematics, and this book will attempt to explain it in this manner.

Many people who consider themselves moderately venturesome invest only in "blue chip" stocks, feeling that in this way they can benefit from optimistic markets without losing too much in pessimistic markets. My philosophy is different. I divide my savings into two parts:

1. A speculative part, which I enjoy having fun with, and
2. An untouchable part, which I put into the safest possible investment vehicle.

I feel that this method is better able to benefit from the optimistic swings and to survive severe contractions. The two parts are not necessarily equal. When you are young and own the capital of a long and healthy life to be lived, you may wish to stress the speculative more; when you are older you may feel less venturesome.

The methods described in this book are not guaranteed to produce a profit; there is no speculation, or even investment, without risk. But I find the financial world exciting and profitable, and it can be so for you, too.

SELECTING A COMPUTER

The kinds of processing described in this book make modest demands on the computer, and if you already have one it will probably be adequate. In case you do not, here are some tips. I will not go into great detail; small computers are developing so rapidly that details would be obsolete in a few months anyway.

I like to be able to print out my programs and data and to plot graphs of my data. Most of all, I like to save my programs and data in a cheap mass memory, and the cheapest I know of is a tape cassette. It takes time to "read" a cassette, and a disk is faster; but so far, tape cassettes are considerably cheaper. If the computer is to have a very small internal memory (for economy) then it is useful for it to have at least two mass memory interfaces so that it can read data in from one, process it, and read it out on the other. Then, with a different program, it can print out or plot the processed data on paper. This *does* take time, which can be saved by investing more in the computer.

It is very desirable for your computer to be able to accept purchased software such as the Fast Fourier transform, and also market price data in purchased form. I punched my own on IBM cards, and it took several hundred hours.

Visit the computer store, look, ask advice, but don't buy on your first or second visit. Buy copies of all the computer magazines in the store, and a couple of books; they will save you money in the long run. Also, consider subscribing to Cycles and joining the Microcomputer Investors Association (addresses are in the Preface).

2
Trends and Averages

In the country of the blind, the one-eyed man is king.
MICHAEL APOSTOLIUS, PROVERBS.

The motivation in looking for uptrends is to catch another Litton on the upswing or to find another budding Xerox. We study trends in the hope that they can (1) get us on the bandwagon early, and (2) tell us when to get off.

The idea is to compare (often by plotting) the current price of a security against its past price to see whether it is trending up or down—or nowhere. The usual practice, though, is to use a *moving average* for the past price. Apparently it is felt that averaging makes the historical price more reliable. Zahorchek[1] goes even further by comparing three moving averages against each other—short-term, medium-term and long-term.

Zahorchek and many others have written about the use of moving averages in guiding investments and speculations. I will not repeat their material here but will proceed to describe what moving averages are, what they mean, and how they can be calculated.

A *time series* is a sequence of numbers representing how the value of a quantity changes with the passage of time. Examples are the daily temperature or the daily price of a security or commodity.

The purpose of *averaging* is to obtain a number which represents the entire time interval and to suppress short-term fluctuations. For example, to find out whether this year was colder than usual, the daily fluctuations of temperature are removed by averaging them out. The average is a good number for representing the entire year.

The *average* value, is calculated by adding all the individual numbers and then dividing that total by the number of numbers added.

MOVING AVERAGES

The moving average does not extend over the entire time series, but only goes back a fixed amount, such as six months. All the data in that span of time are figured into the moving average. As time goes by the moving average "slides" along; each time a new data point becomes available it is included in the new average, and the oldest data point is dropped. Figure 2–1 shows the *memory* of the moving average (b) and of the ordinary average (a) for comparison.

There are two different ways to use the moving average:

1. You may wish to compare the smoothed output of the moving average with the raw data. Figure 2–2 shows an example of this. In the figure, the raw data is on top (a) and I have postulated a "V" shape in it, like a selling climax which depressed the price

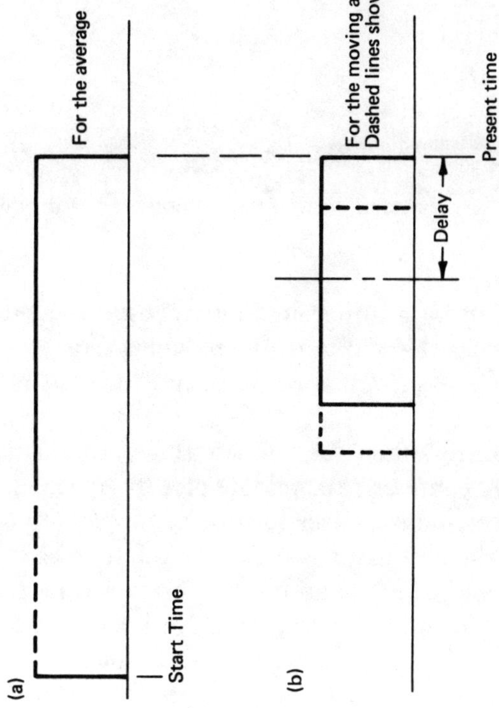

FIGURE 2-1. "Memory" of the average (a) and the moving average (b).

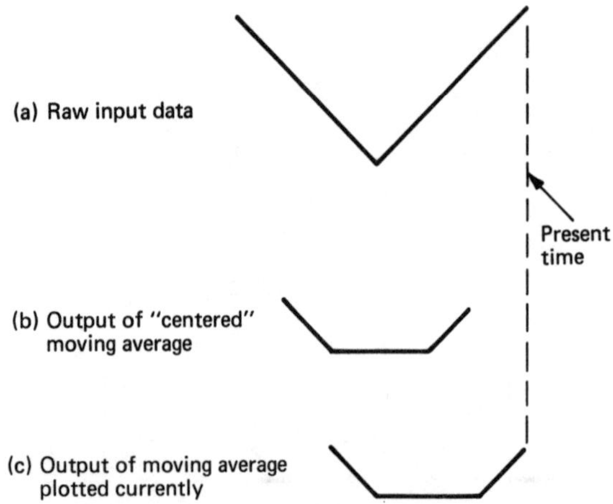

FIGURE 2-2. The raw data (a) and the moving average (b and c).

followed by a turnaround and recovery. The middle plot (b) is the output of the moving average.

There is a *delay* in the output of the moving average, equal to one-half its span; that is, if the span is six months, then the delay is three months. Therefore, I "centered" the middle plot by moving it back by three months. The purpose of this centering is to make the best match with the raw data so as to trace cause and effect relationships through from the raw data into the smoothed data. Notice that the point of the "V" in the raw data came through blunted in the output of the moving average.

2. More frequently, the moving average is plotted currently, as in (c) of Figure 2–2, and is used as the basis for buy and sell rules. A typical method is to plot the raw data and the moving average on the same

chart; if the raw data is above the moving average, then the trend is upward.

To some degree the future course of the moving average is predictable. In Figure 2–2 the "corner" on the right-hand side of the output was generated as the trailing edge of the moving average passed the point of the V in the raw data. There are two alternative ways of dealing with this predictability:

a. You can use the most popular span of time for your moving average, knowing that everyone using that method will then be receiving the same "signals", thus assuring that you will buy popular stocks.

b. You can regard the "trailing edge" effect of the moving average as spurious, and avoid it by using a filter. Filters will be discussed later in this book, beginning with Chapter 4.

To complete this discussion of trends we will discuss the trend of the overall stock market. A market average, or index, is both a measure of the degree of optimism in the market and a "climate" influencing the price action of individual stocks.

The long-term market trend is shown in Figure 2–3. The slope of the solid straight line represents a growth rate of 2.85% per year. However, since the 1930s, part of that growth has been fictitious because it was due to inflation. The dashed line shows the market trend after correction for inflation.

One can make either of two statements about the dashed line. Either our prosperity has seen its best days, or the stock market is about to make a new upward surge. Maybe both are true. This is discussed further in Chapter 7.

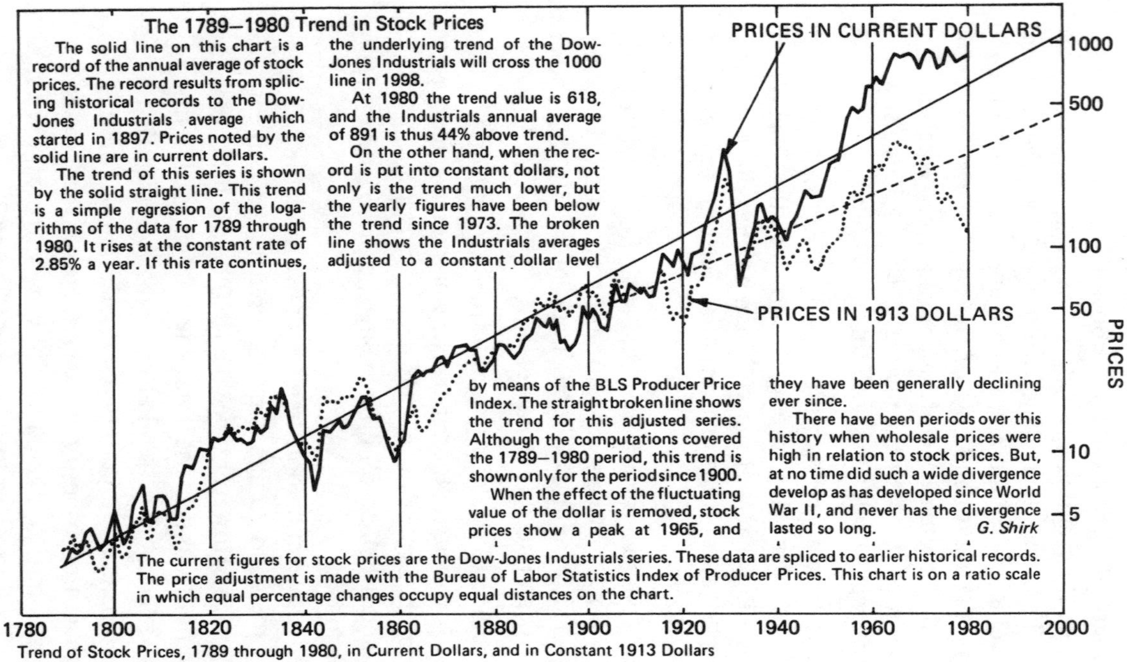

FIGURE 2-3. **Due to inflation, the real value of blue chip stocks has been going down since 1965. Copyright 1981 by Foundation for the Study of Cycles, 124 S. Highland Ave., Pittsburgh, PA 15206 (by permission).**

REFERENCE

1. Zahorchak, Michael G., *The Art of Low-Risk Investing,* Van Nostrand Reinhold, 1977.

3 Fluctuations and Oscillations

There is a tide in the affairs of men . . .
SHAKESPEARE, JULIUS CAESAR.

Someone once asked Bernard Baruch what the stock market was going to do, and his answer was, "It will fluctuate".

Can we use those fluctuations to buy low and sell high? This chapter will describe fluctuations, and the following chapters will describe tools for analyzing them and estimating the best timing for buying and selling.

The financial markets have been studied for a long time, and many respected researchers have reported that the fluctuations are *random*[1]. It would be difficult to make money out of random fluctuations unless you are a broker earning commissions. What I look for is a regular *oscillation* hidden among the random fluctuations. Hurst[2] said in his book that we can make money in the long run by timing our buy and sell actions in accordance with a regular oscillation. Of course, the oscillation has to be large enough to pay the broker's commission to at least break even.

FREQUENCY

A large body of theory has been developed to describe fluctuations. Some of this theory is easy enough to use, but it is easiest to visualize in terms of *frequency*.

Frequency is defined as *alternations per unit of time.* Activity in the construction industry oscillates with a frequency of one cycle per year (Figure 3–1).

You can search for regular oscillations in your time series data by looking at its frequency *spectrum.* You are already familiar with a frequency spectrum—your radio dial. To plot the frequency spectrum of your time series, run it through the Fourier transform (software is available for purchase). Figure 3–2 shows the frequency spectrum of stock prices. The frequency spectrum of a random fluctuation is more or less smooth (it will have random fluctuations). If the spectrum of your time series is flat, it may not contain any oscillations large enough for use. A strong regular oscillation will show up as a distinct peak in the spectrum.

You do not have to do all this prospecting work yourself. If you prefer, you can read about the work of others in Cycles magazine. They search for cycles in many areas.

But finding such a peak in the spectrum is not enough—you still need to know when to buy and sell. You need to examine your oscillation in more detail. You need a *filter* to reject the random fluctuations and display your oscillation more clearly. Much of the remainder of this book is concerned with filters, beginning with the next chapter.

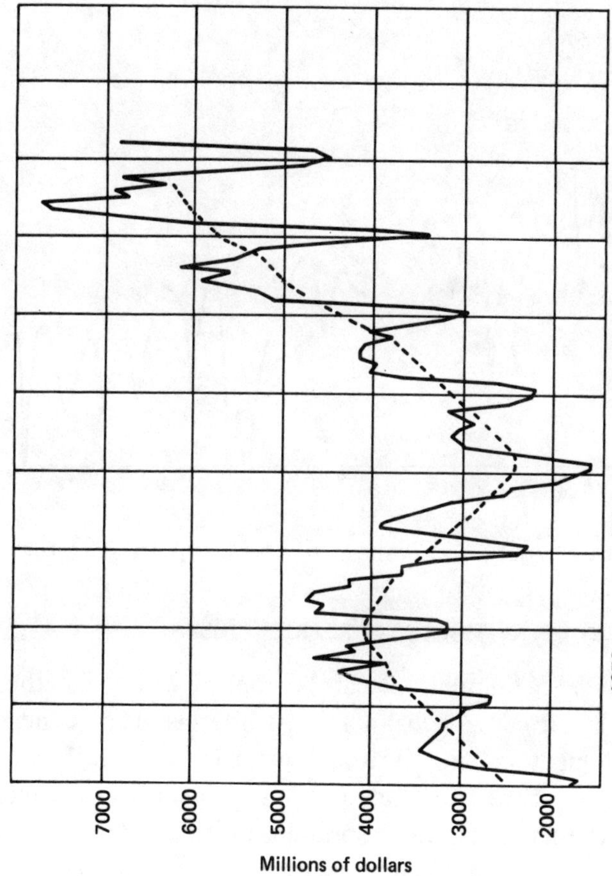

FIGURE 3–1. Activity in the construction industry oscillates once per year. By Gertrude Shirk, copyright 1979 by Foundation for the Study of Cycles, 124 S. Highland Ave., Pittsburgh, PA 15206 (by permission).

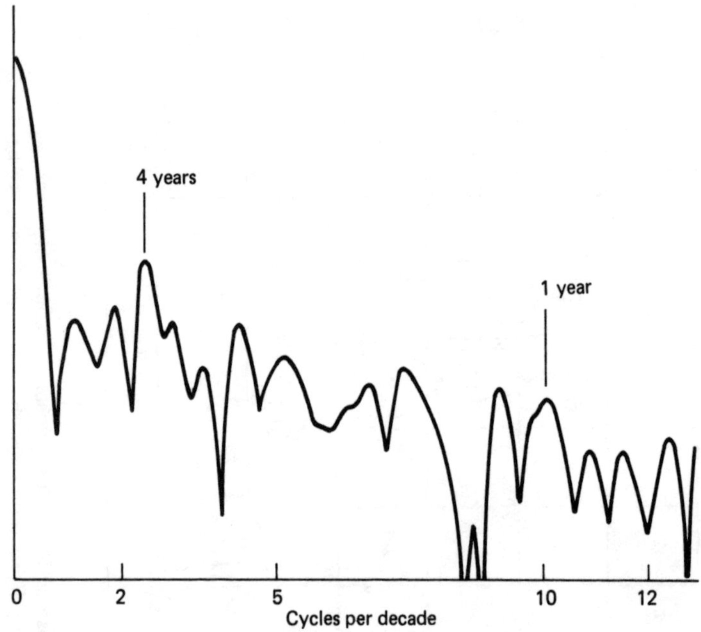

FIGURE 3-2. Frequency spectrum of stock prices (DJIA) since 1948.

THINKING FREQUENCIES

The theory of fluctuations can be applied without mathematics, but it comes most naturally in terms of frequency. An example to support this statement is shown in Figure 3–3, a plot of the frequency response of a moving average. On the left-hand side the response is plotted versus period, and on the right-hand side versus frequency. Both plots show exactly the same data, because frequency is the inverse of period: $f = 1/t$. However, the right-hand plot shows more clearly the frequencies of the nulls, since they occur at integral multiples. Other examples will occur throughout this book, and they all argue in favor of the frequency viewpoint.

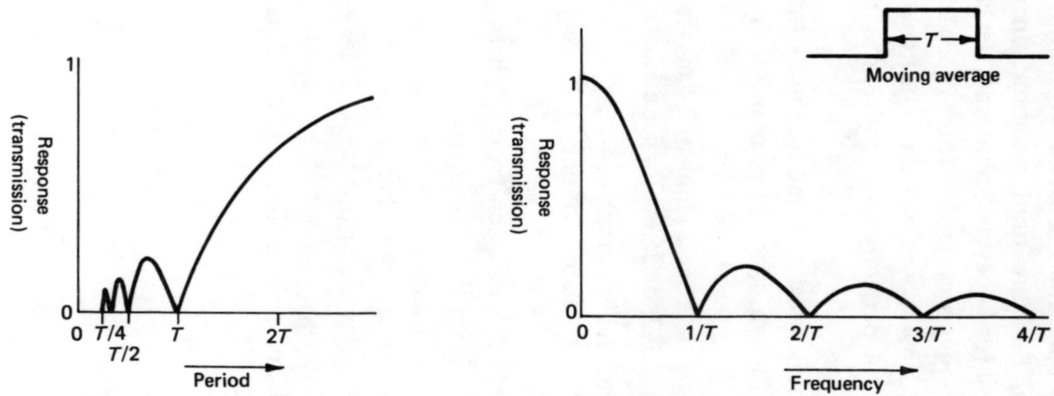

FIGURE 3.3 The frequency response of a moving average. The left-hand plot is versus period, and the right-hand plot is versus frequency. Most theoretical relationships are easier to see when plotted versus frequency.

But many people find it difficult to think in terms of frequency when they are thinking about financial data. Cycles per second (or kilocycles, or megacycles) are all very well, but what about a cycle that takes four *years* to complete its period? How do we think about its frequency–0.25 cycles per year? A perfectly valid concept, but awkward, isn't it?

The problem is a real one, and I do not know a perfect solution. I will, though, suggest two useful techniques:

1. Use a longer time base: Think of 2.5 cycles per decade as in Figure 3–2, or 25 cycles per century.
2. Think of an oscillation with a 4-year period as an oscillation with a frequency of one cycle every four years.

Still awkward, isn't it? I don't suggest that you break up your Kiwanis luncheon to talk of cycles per century; this is merely an exercise to bend your brains into the proper attitude when you encounter phenomena like modulation and nonlinearity later on in this book. It may take some mental effort and practise, but if you seriously want to analyze investments for years to come, it will pay off.

REFERENCES

1. Cootner, P., *The Random Character of Stock Market Prices,* MIT Press, 1964.
2. Hurst, J.M., *The Profit Magic of Stock Transaction Timing,* Prentice-Hall, 1970.

4
An Introduction to Filters

Never reason from what you do not know.
ANDREW MICHAEL RAMSEY

A digital filter is a set of numbers used by a computer to operate on time series data in order to produce a filtered output time series. These numbers are applied according to a specific *algorithm* (procedure). Example algorithms will be described in detail in the following two chapters.

The purpose of filtering is to separate the fluctuations of different frequencies from each other. A rapid fluctuation contains high frequencies, and a slow, smooth undulation contains low frequencies. More precisely, filtering suppresses undesired frequencies in order to expose desired frequencies for study. It is possible for an oscillation to be large enough to be significant, yet still be buried in random "noise" and hidden by it. Filtering can bring out such an oscillation by reducing the amplitude of the unwanted frequencies.

You can buy software for the Fourier transform. This will analyze your time series data and plot its frequency spectrum (Chapter 9). Then why would anyone fool around with digital filters? The problem is that an oscillation might not go on forever without change. I suspect that many of them change frequently, and you need to know that if you are going to put your money on them. The Fourier transform only shows that it is there; by then using digital filters you can watch it change.

LOW PASS AND HIGH PASS FILTERS

A filter that suppresses high frequencies and passes low frequencies on through to the output is called a *low pass* filter. Conversely, a filter which suppresses low frequencies and passes high frequencies on through is called a *high pass* filter. Figure 4–1(a) shows the frequency response of a low pass filter, and Figure 4–1(b) shows the frequency response of a high pass filter.

Figure 4–2 is a time series plot of an index of stock prices. The upper and lower plots represent a single time series after being passed through digital filters. What the filtering did was to separate the high frequencies from the low frequencies, and each is shown in its own separate plot.

It is possible to reject the high frequencies and the low frequencies at the same time; the result is called a band pass filter.

Actually, the moving average discussed in Chapter 2 is one form of low pass filter, but we want a better tool. Figure 2–2 in Chapter 2 showed how the "trailing edge" effect introduced a spurious wiggle in the smoothed output data. In the frequency domain, Figure 3–3 shows the awkwardness of the moving average if we should use it as a filter: the frequency response contains ripples. Sometimes these effects are acceptable, but it is easy enough to remove them by designing the filter properly. These methods will be explained in Chapters 5 and 6.

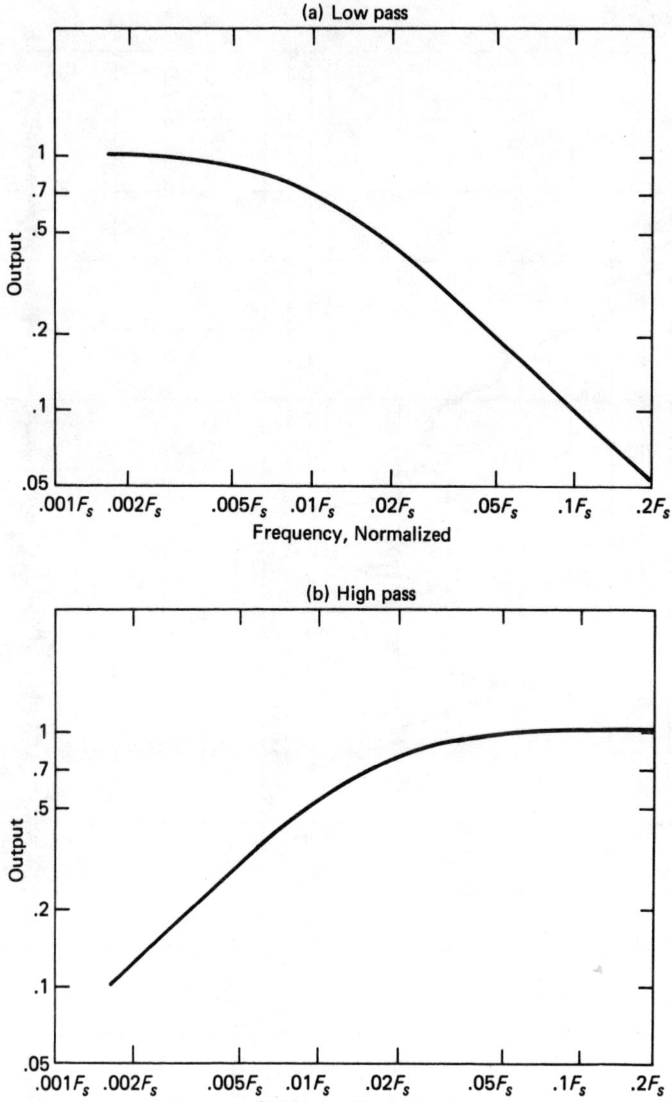

FIGURE 4-1. Frequency response of filters.

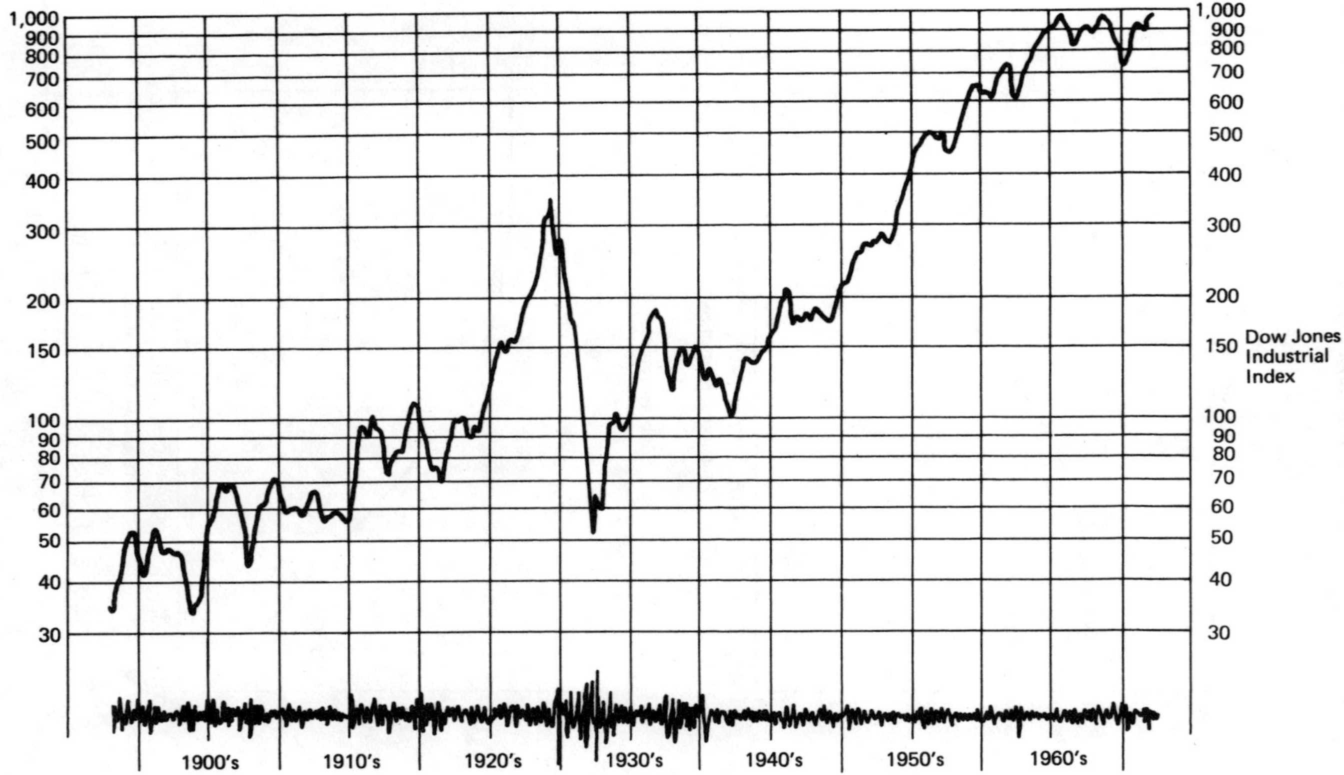

FIGURE 4-2. Stock price index after filtering. The low frequencies are in the top curve, and the high frequencies are along the bottom.

DIGITAL FILTERS

We turn now to the structure of digital filters. For our purposes, there are two kinds of digital filters—feedback filters and feedforward filters.

A feedback filter works by taking part of its output data and feeding that back to its input. In a feed-forward-only filter, that is not done; only the raw input data is operated on to produce the output.

It is possible to use both feedback and feed-forward methods in the same filter. In fact, that is frequently done in designing communication filters which need to have very steep "skirts" in order to reject adjacent-channel interference. (Filters of that kind are designed by sophisticated mathematical methods which are not discussed in this book.)

At first glance, steep-sided filters seem attractive for securities analysis too; but the trouble is they can *generate* oscillations in the data. We certainly do not want to invest in an oscillation that is not really there.

The advantages and disadvantages of each type of filter are listed below:

Computer power required—The feedback filter requires less computer power.

Timing—The feed-forward-only filter has the same time lag at all frequencies.* If your purpose is to compare the filtered data with the raw data, then this will be convenient.

---

*Provided that the filter is symmetrical, that is, its trailing edge is a mirror image of its leading edge.

Stability—Feedback filters can be unstable and *generate* oscillations if they are not properly designed. The chapter on feedback filters will tell how this can be avoided.

The following two chapters will describe the two types of filters in more detail and how to design them.

5
Feed-Forward-Only Filters

HOW A FILTER WORKS

A low pass filter is a set of multiplying constants which, when added, equal 1 (unity), together with a suitable algorithm for using them in the proper sequence (Figure 5–1). The filter contains enough of these multipliers to cover the smoothing span required.

The moving average is a type of filter. If the filter is intended to calculate the moving average, then all the multiplying constants are equal; but in the usual case they will be tapered as will be discussed later.

To form each data point in the smoothed output, the recent raw input data points are multiplied by the filter numbers, each individually by each, and the results are added. This sum becomes one point in the smoothed output data. Figure 5–2 shows this process. The top row of vertical lines represents the raw data input time series, and the middle row represents the filter numbers. The length of each line represents the value of the number it stands for. Now, multiply each raw data point in the top row by the filter number immediately below it, and add up all these products. The sum is a smoothed output data point, and is shown plotted as a black dot.

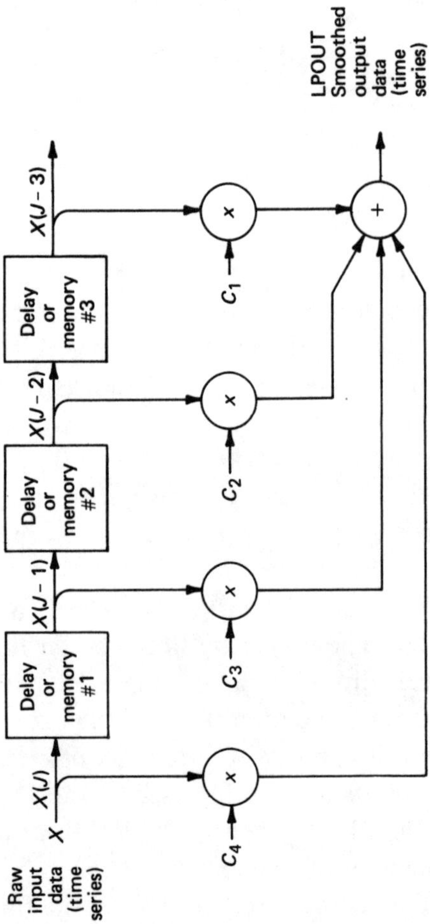

FIGURE 5-1. Signal flow diagram of filter. The circles show arithmetic operations as indicated. The *'C's'* are the filter numbers; they add up to 1 (unity). If all the *C's* are equal, the output is the moving average.

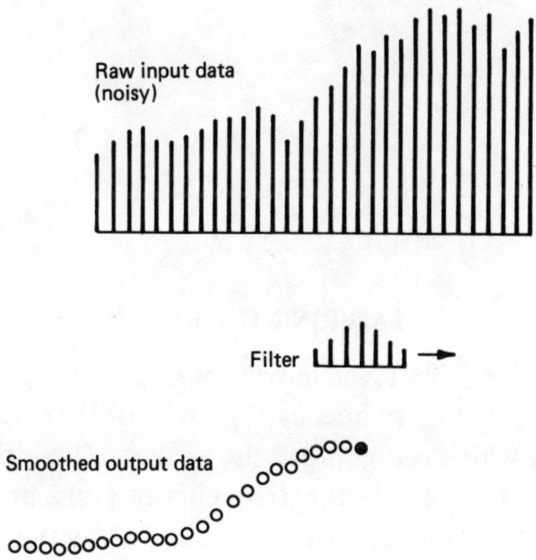

FIGURE 5-2. How a digital filter works.

Next, the filter is moved one interval to the right to take in a newer point, and in doing so it releases an old point on its left. The multiplying and adding are now repeated. This process of multiplying, adding, and sliding one data interval to repeat the process is called the *convolution summation.* It is continued until the raw data points have all been used. The smoothed output data points for past times are shown as tiny circles.

A FORTRAN program for a digital filter is shown below.

```
C     X ARE THE RAW INPUT DATA POINTS
C     C ARE THE FILTER CONSTANTS
C     LPOUT ARE THE SMOOTHED OUTPUT POINTS
```

```
          DO 13 J=23,3927
          LPOUT (J) = 0
          I=J
          DO 8 K=1,23
          LPOUT (J) = LPOUT (J) + C(K) * X(I)
          I=I-1
8         CONTINUE
13        CONTINUE
```

TAPERING THE FILTER

As a low pass filter, the moving average is not perfect. The trouble is that its frequency response contains ripples (Figure 5–3) which can confuse the analyst. These ripples can be reduced and a smoother frequency response produced by shaping the filter. The ripples are caused by the abrupt beginning and end of the moving average filter and can be reduced by rounding or tapering* the edges of the filter (Fig-

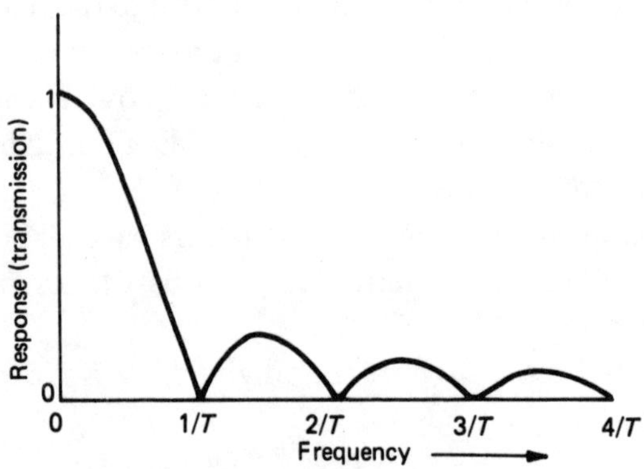

FIGURE 5-3. As a filter, the moving average is not ideal because its response contains ripples.

---

*A similar effect can be obtained by taking a moving average of a moving average (see references 2 and 3).

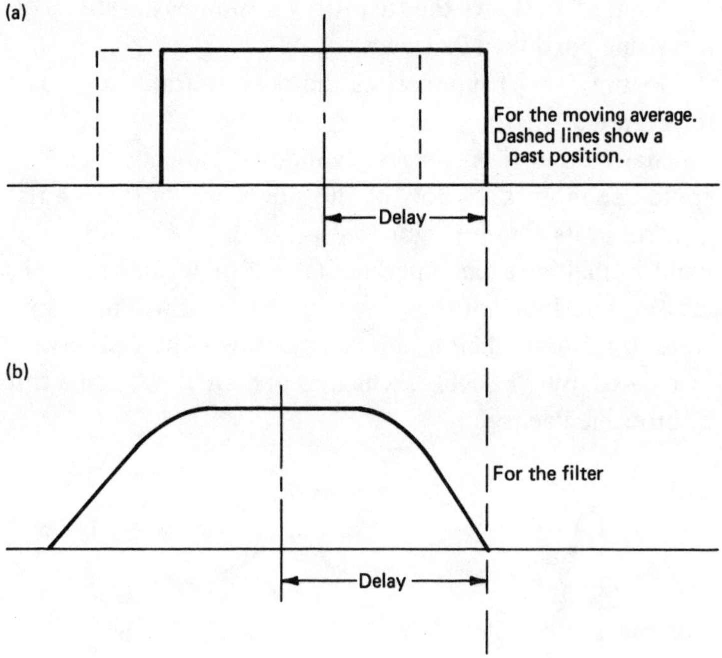

FIGURE 5-4. "Memory" of the moving average (a) and of a tapered filter (b).

ure 5–4). The improvement is shown in Figure 5–5. Curve A represents the moving average, repeated here for comparison. Curve B represents a trapezoidal filter with steep edges, and curve C represents more gradually sloping edges. In curve D the top of the trapezoid has disappeared and the filter envelope has become a triangle.

Figure 5–6(b) shows how the largest spurious peak varies with the shape of the trapezoid. Making the edges slope more gradually reduces this spurious peak until it passes through a minimum for shape C. This could be called a "tuning" effect.

Figure 5–7 shows the frequency responses of various filters using portions of a sine wave.

Figure 5–8(b) summarizes the peak spurious responses for Figure 5–7.

Many other filter shapes ("windows") are possible. You could use more than 360° of the sine wave, or insert a flat portion in its center (Figure 5–9). You have virtually a free hand in making such experiments, and they can be fun. To see the side lobes of the filters you try, you will need software to calculate their Fourier transforms. (These plots were calculated by "FORIT", which is part of IBM's Scientific Subroutine Package.)

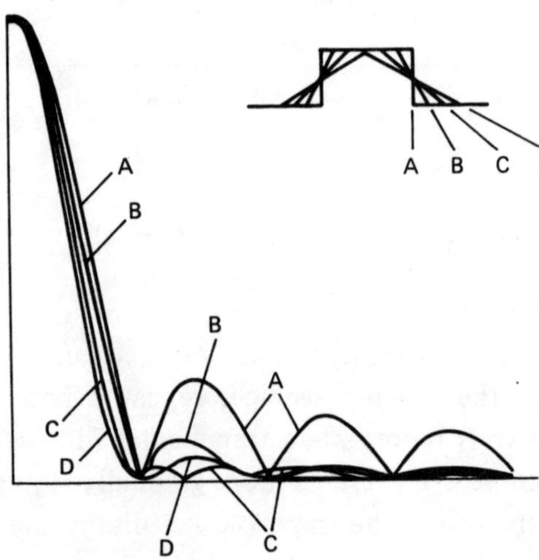

FIGURE 5-5. Frequency responses of filters having trapezoidal shapes (straight, sloping sides).

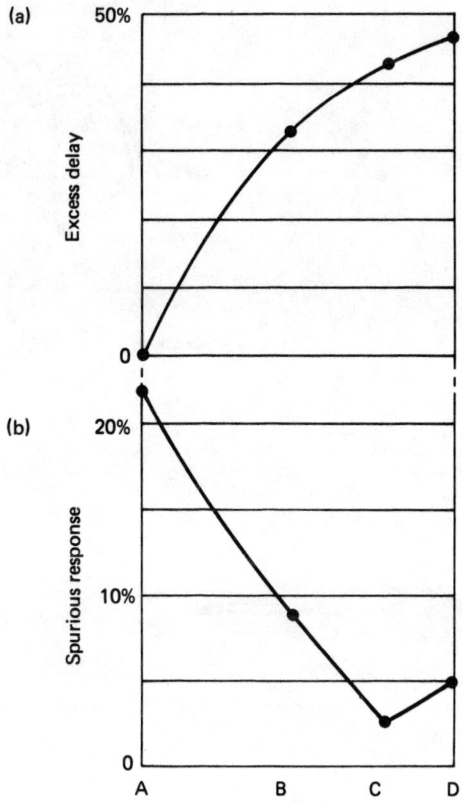

FIGURE 5-6(a). Excess span and delay, relative to the moving average.

FIGURE 5-6(b). Spurious response of the filters in Figure 5-5.

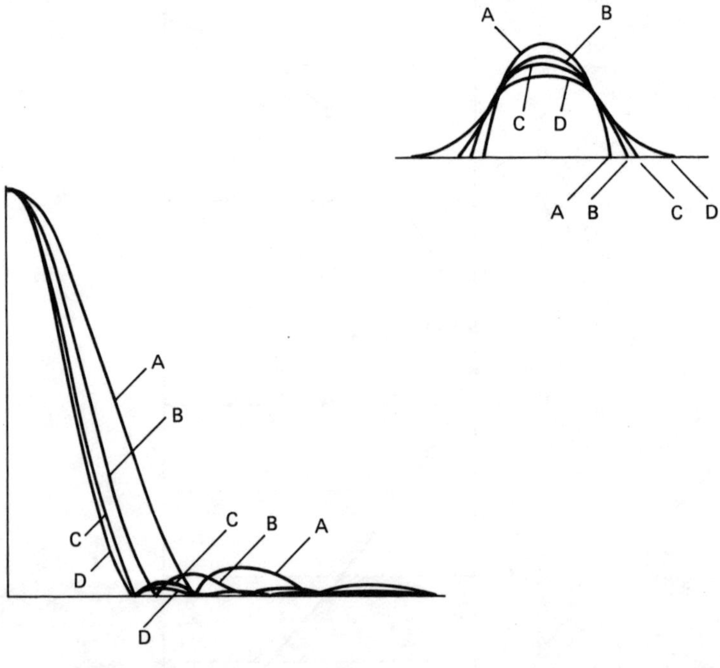

FIGURE 5-7. Frequency responses of filters whose shapes are various portions of a sine wave.

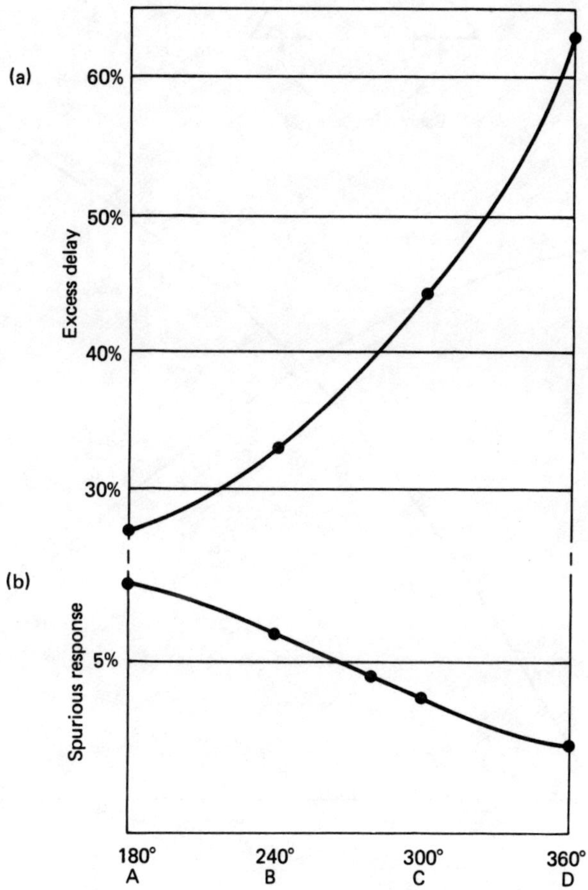

FIGURE 5-8(a). **Excess span and delay, relative to the moving average.**

FIGURE 5-8(b). **Spurious response of the sine wave filters in Figures 5-6.**

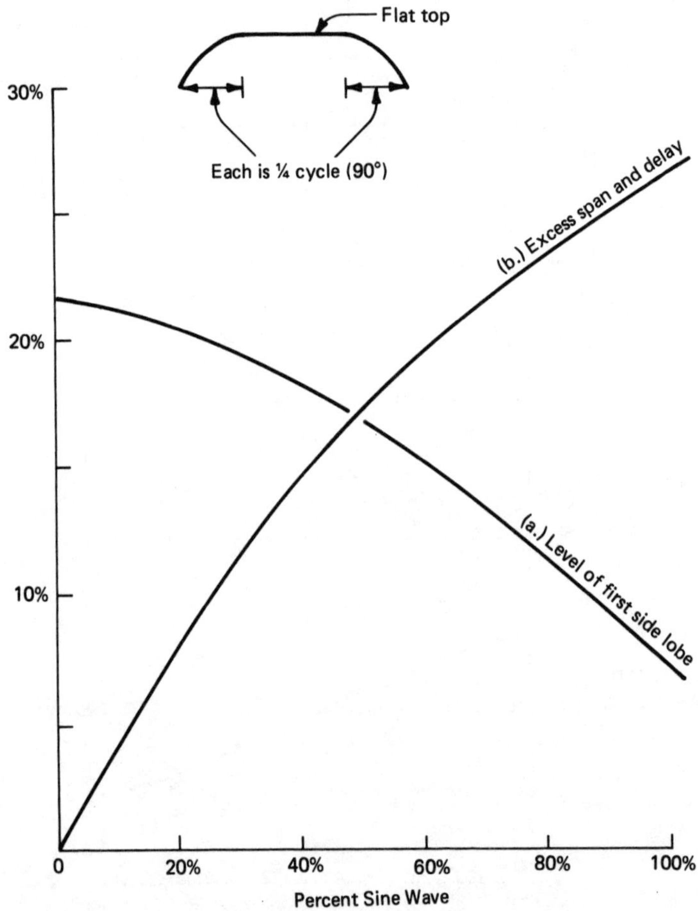

FIGURE 5-9. Spurious response (a) and excess delay (b) of a flat-topped sine wave filter. [At 0% sine wave the flat-top degenerates into the moving average.]

FILTER DELAY

When we try to improve one aspect of performance, Nature often retaliates by degrading some other aspect. In filters, one price of smoother frequency response is greater delay as we saw in Figure 5–4. The output of a symmetrical filter is delayed by half the span of the filter. Figures 5–6(a), 5–8(a), and 5–9(b) show the excess span length (and delay) required for the different filters as compared with the moving average. The comparison is based on the same filtering capability as the moving average; that is, they all have the same bandwidth at the half-amplitude frequency.

Thus, the choice of filter shape is a compromise. If the extra delay is no drawback in the particular application at hand, then we can choose a filter mostly for its smooth frequency response. But if we are working with "real-time" data and don't want to lose the most recent results, then we can choose a filter with a shorter span and accept some ripples in the response.

The three types of filters are compared in Figure 5–10, which shows them all in one plot. The all-around "best" type would be the one that is nearest to the lower left-hand corner; the half sine wave looks pretty good.

The numbers used in some of these filters are listed in the appendix of this chapter.

The rule given above for the delay—"half the span"—is strictly true only for symmetrical filters; that is, their leading and trailing edges are mirror images of each other. The filters described in this chapter are all symmetrical. The advantage of symmetrical filters is that their delay is independent of frequency. This makes it easier to compare the filtered output with unfiltered data. However, there is a

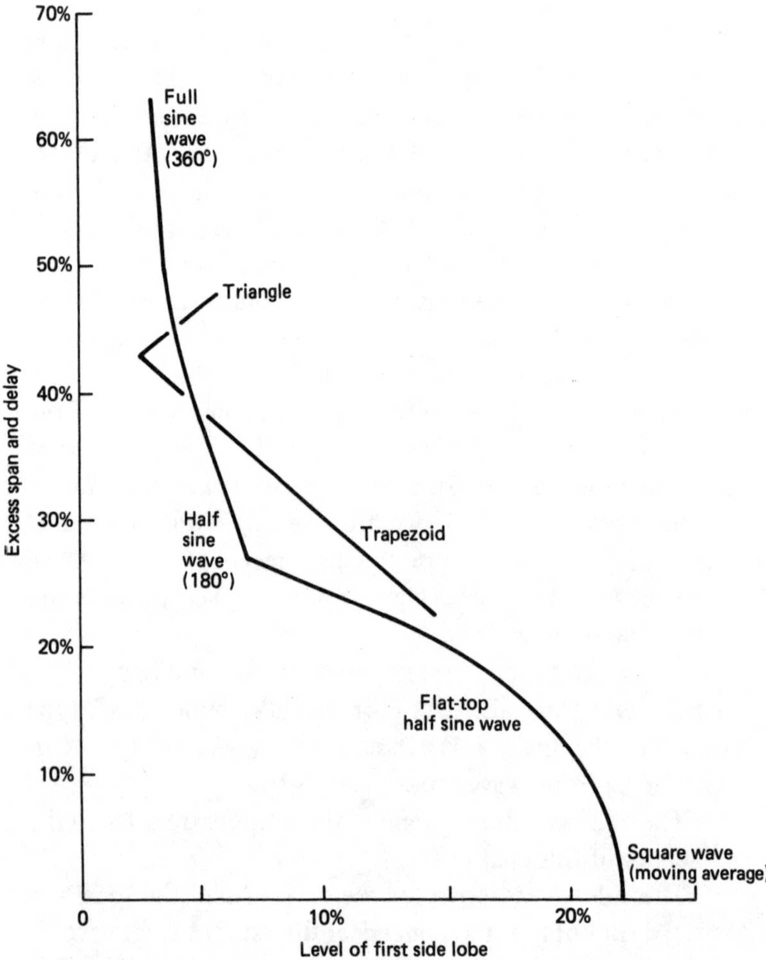

FIGURE 5-10. Summary of the properties of the three types of symmetrical filter shapes.

penalty. Symmetrical filters have more delay than do filters which weight the recent data more heavily.

CENTERING

In Figure 5–2, note that the smoothed filter output dot was plotted under the *center* of the filter; that is, not under the most recent raw data point, but back-spaced from it by the amount of the filter delay. This is the proper way to line up the output of the filter with the raw data when you wish to compare the two. If you like, you can separate the raw data into several different frequency bands, or intervals, and plot them all one beneath the other. This would be the way to align them for comparison, that is, adjust each by the amount of its filter delay. Then you can compare them all directly with each other.

Assigning dates to your filtered data is discussed in the appendix of this chapter.

Centering is not the only way to plot the filtered output. Often you will see it plotted currently. In this case, it is not so easy to compare directly with the raw data (though you can make the adjustment mentally if you wish). The motivation for plotting the smoothed data currently is for trend detection; this was discussed in Chapter 2.

STEPS IN DESIGNING A SMOOTHING FILTER

1. Choose the effective smoothing span required for sufficient smoothing. A span of 19 weeks was used in generating Figure 5–11.

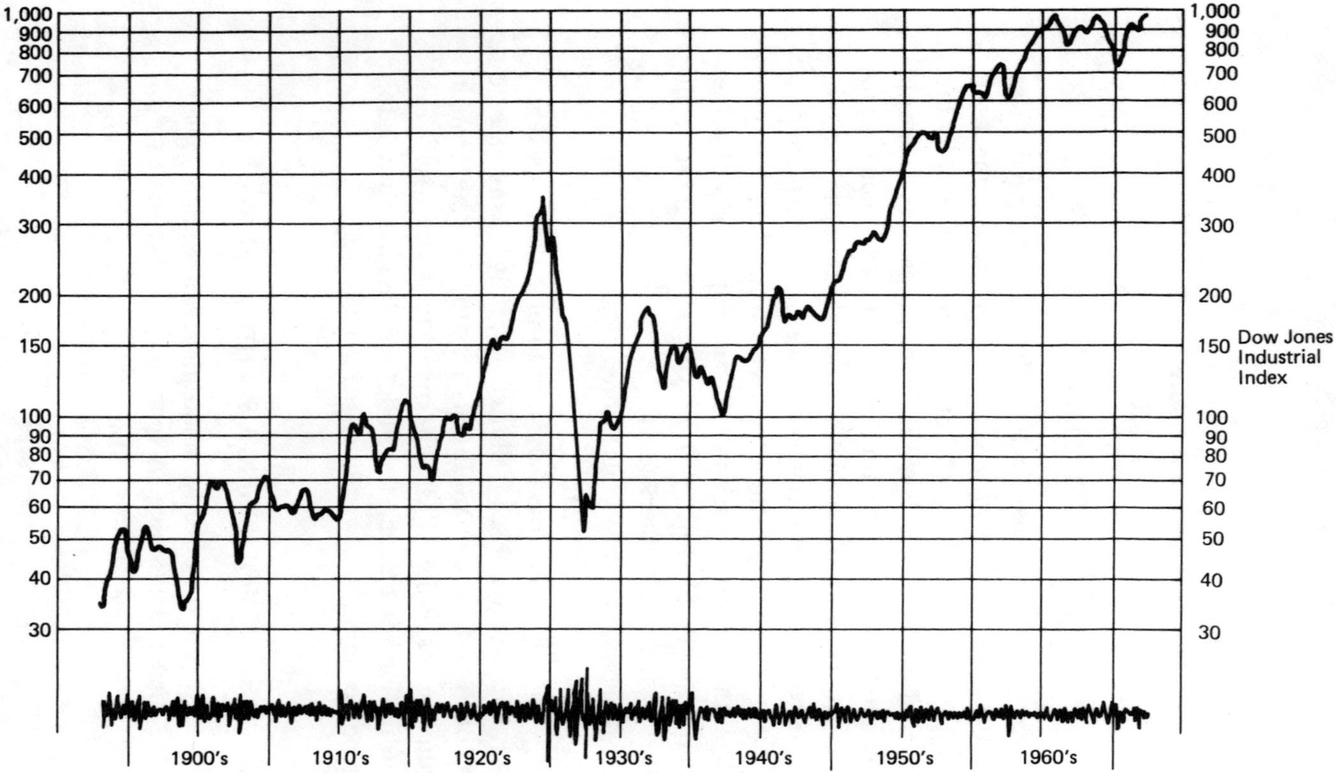

FIGURE 5-11. Stock price index after filtering. The low frequencies are in the top curve, and the high frequencies are along the bottom.

2. Choose a filter shape for an appropriate compromise between smoothness of frequency response and excess filter delay, by reference to Figures 5-5 through 5-10 or other information. The filter used in generating Figure 5-11 had a half-sine-wave envelope. Figure 5-8 shows that this filter has a peak spurious response of 7.3% and an excess delay of 27%. The delay is half the span.
3. The total span of the filter is the effective span chosen in step 1, plus the excess span required for the shape chosen in step 2. The total span used for Figure 5-11 was 24 weeks.
4. The number of constants required in the filter equals the total span divided by the time interval between data samples, plus 1. The time interval is 1 week, so 25 constants were required in this filter. (The first and last constants were zero and were omitted; the filter actually contained 23 constants.) An odd number of constants is convenient because then the delay is an integral number of data intervals. (In Figure 5-11, the input data consisted of weekly averages of the daily closing DJI Index.)
5. Assign tentative values to the individual filter constants in accordance with the filter shape chosen in step 2. These values were simply read from a table of natural sines at 7.5° intervals.
6. Adjust the values of the filter constants to add-up to unity. To do this, add all the tentative values found in step 5 and divide each constant by the total. The actual filter values used are shown in the appendix of this chapter.

HIGH PASS FILTERS

So far we have discussed smoothing (low pass) filters only, so called because they suppress the high frequencies and pass the low frequencies, as shown in Figure 4–1(a). High pass filters do the opposite—the low frequencies are suppressed and the high frequencies are passed, as in Figure 4–1(b). A high pass filter is shown in Figure 5–12. To visualize how this works, understand that a "filter" consisting of the single constant unity simply passes the input data through to the output, unaltered. To form a high pass filter, we subtract a low pass filter from the unity filter. The resulting filter looks like Figure 5–12, which cancels out the low frequencies but leaves (passes) the highs.

Alternatively, the raw data can be smoothed by a plain low pass filter like the one shown in Figure 5–2, and then the smoothed output can be subtracted from the raw input

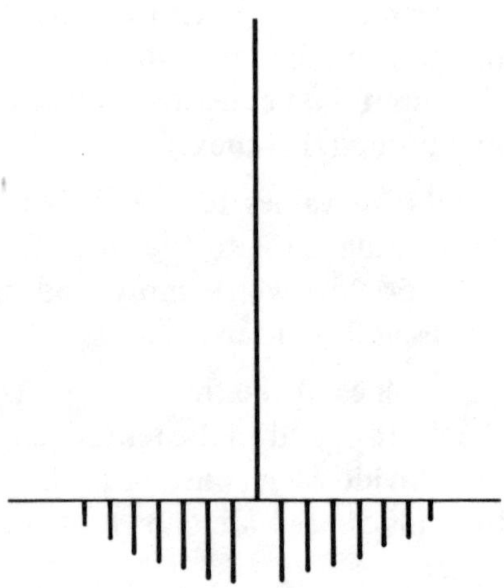

FIGURE 5-12. The numbers in a high pass filter.

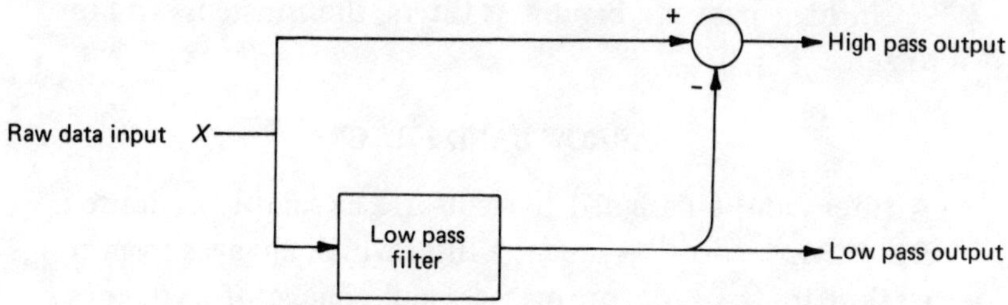

FIGURE 5-13. Changing a low pass filter into a high pass filter.

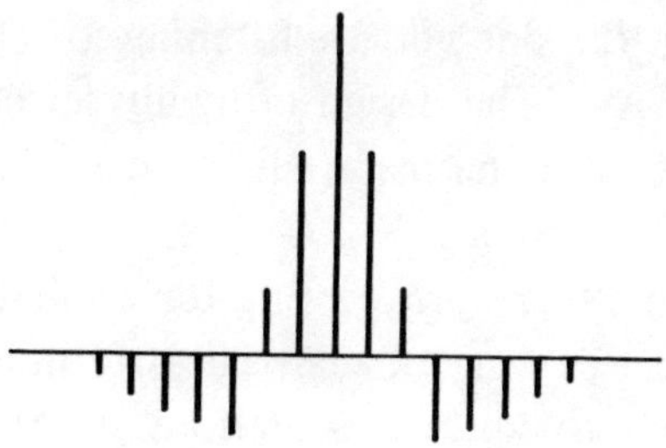

FIGURE 5-14. The numbers in a (broad) band pass filter.

data in a second step, as shown in Figure 5–13. The two methods are mathematically equivalent, and their results are the same.

BAND PASS FILTERS

A band (region) of frequencies can be isolated by suppressing both low and high frequencies. Suppose that in Figure 5–11 we wished to suppress the week-to-week fluctuations as well as the low frequency fluctuations. This can be done with the filter sketched in Figure 5–14. This band pass filter resembles the high pass filter of Figure 5–12 except that the unity constant has been replaced by a 5-term low pass filter.

In high pass and band pass filters, the constants add up to zero.

NARROW BAND FILTERS

A filter can be designed to "cut-off" as sharply as desired. By "sharp cut-off" is meant a filter which changes from rejection to transmission over a small change of frequency. The filters in your radio and TV sets are of this type, so that you can tune in a station clearly without interference from dozens of signals on other channels, some of them much stronger than the one you are listening to. This property is called selectivity. (The design of highly selective digital filters is described in the materials listed in Further Reading at the end of the book.)

But when we are prospecting for oscillations in a data series, we must be wary of sharp cut-off filters because their output is likely to contain oscillations. We can explain these oscillations by saying the filter is resonant. Or we can say that by restricting the width of the spectrum transmitted, the filter prolongs the response after an impulse by ringing.

The two explanations are equivalent; in any case you can see the oscillatory nature of a narrow-band filter in Figure 5–15. This filter was designed in accordance with Reference 1 and incorporates unitary filters of orders 4 and 5 of an 11th-order filter.

REJECTION FILTERS

Figure 5-3 showed that the ordinary moving average has a "null" (zero response) at certain frequencies, and much of this chapter was devoted to methods for reducing the size of the "ripples". At this point in our discussion, it is ap-

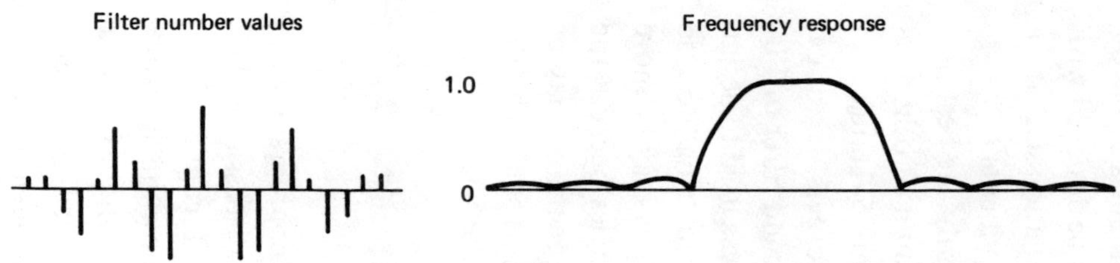

FIGURE 5-15. Narrow-band filter.

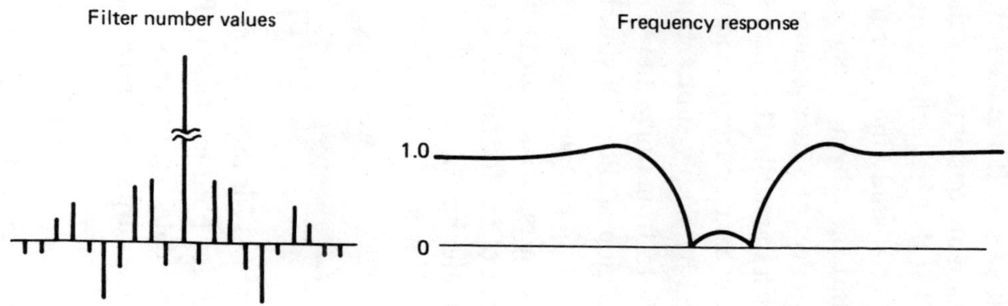

FIGURE 5-16. Narrow-band rejection filter.

propriate to ask whether the nulls are always undesirable; perhaps they can be useful in data analysis. The answer is a qualified yes. If the data are found to contain a stable oscillation of constant frequency, a filter can be designed with a null at that frequency to remove the oscillation so that we can better study the other frequency components.

But the moving average is not necessarily the best possible rejection filter because it attenuates a lot of other frequencies as well. The filter shown in Figure 5–16 rejects a narrow band of frequencies and passes all others. It was designed by simply subtracting the narrow-band filter of Figure 5–15 from unity, the same trick that was used to design the high-pass filter. Obviously, this filter can "ring" too, so use it with care; however, narrow-band filters may be more useful in rejecting than in passing frequencies because the output of the former, covering a broader spectrum, may be of greater amplitude so that an oscillation introduced by the filter is less troublesome. It depends on the nature of the data being analyzed.

A COMPUTER PROGRAM

Figure 5–17 is the flow chart for a computer program which produces both low pass (LPOUT) and high pass (HPOUT) output data. The program itself is listed in Figure 5–18.

The purpose of a flow chart is to show how the operation of the program is controlled as it steps through the raw data. This is in contrast to a signal (data) flow block diagram, such as in Figure 5–1, which follows the data through the various algorithms and explains how they function. For example, Figure 5–1 shows the filtering process as a parallel action, and it shows clearly what makes the filter perform as it does.

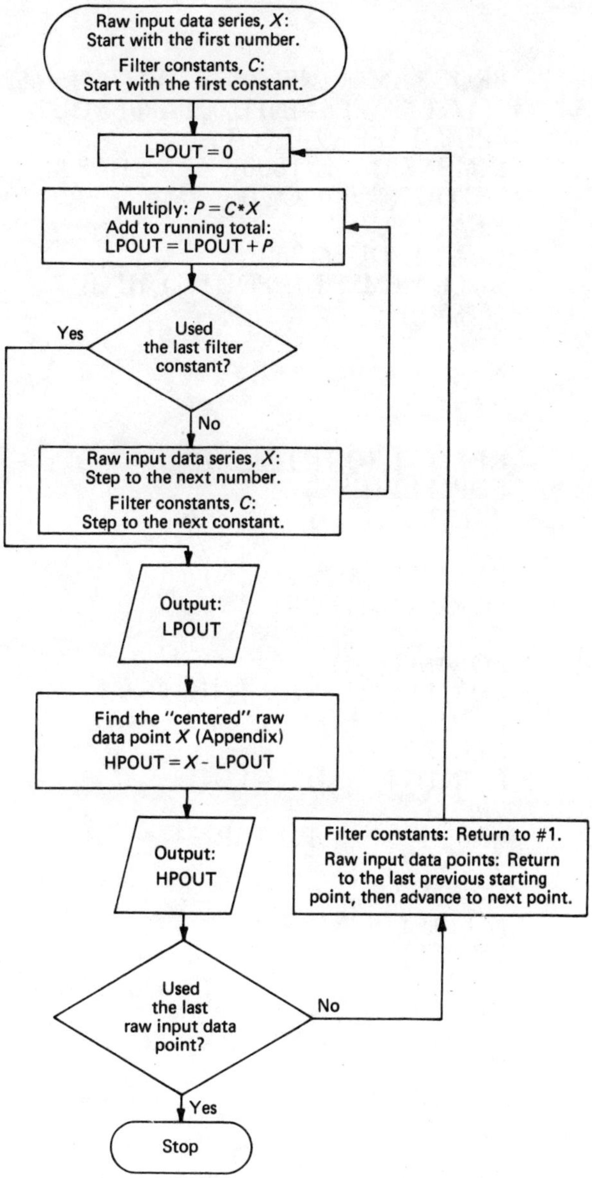

FIGURE 5-17. Flow chart for filter.

```
          PROGRAM H(INPUT=65, OUTPUT=65,
         1 PLOT, TAPE5=INPUT, TAPE6=OUT-
         1 PUT, TAPE 19=PLOT)
          DIMENSION  X(1800),  LPOUT(1800),
         1 HPOUT(1800), C(200)
          REAL LPOUTT
          REAL LPOUT(1800)
          CALL MEMSET (HPOUT(1), HPOUT
         1 (1800))
C
          NF = 23
          N = 1800
C
          READ 21, (C(J), J = 1, NF)
   21     FORMAT (F8.6)
          PRINT 21, (C(J), J = 1, NF)
C
          READ 25, (X(J), J = 1,N)
   25     FORMAT (10F6.4)
C
   35     FORMAT(1H1)
   44     FORMAT (1H, 5F 9.4, 1H, 5F 9.4)
   46     FORMAT(1H, 5F10.6, 4X, 5F10.6)
          PRINT 35
          PRINT 44, (X(J), J = 1, N)
C
C                      FILTER
C
          NC = N - NF
          DO I03 I=1, NC
          LPOUTT = 0
          I1 = I
          DO 104 K = 1, NF
          LPOUTT=LPOUTT+C(K)*X(I1)
          I1 = I1 + 1
  104     CONTINUE
          I0 = I + NF/2
          LPOUT(IO) = LPOUTT
          HPOUT(IO) = X(IO) - LPOUTT
```

```
103     CONTINUE
C
        PRINT 35
        PRINT 46, (LPOUT(J), J = 1,N)
        PRINT 35
        PRINT 46, (HPOUT(J), J = 1,N)
C
C
C                      PLOT
C
        CALL PLOTSQ(0, 0, 19)
        CALL OBJEG(.8, 0.5, 42.0, 4.7)
        CALL PAGE
        CALL SUBJEG(0. -0.174, 1800., 0.174)
        CALL LINEG1(1800, HPOUT, 1., 1.)
        CALL EXITG
        STOP
        END
```

FIGURE 5-18. Filtering program (FORTRAN).

However, it is more economical to operate most computers in a serial mode, multiplying the data numbers one at a time and adding the products; the result is the same. The flow chart (Figure 5-17) shows how this can be accomplished.

REFERENCES

1. Craddock. J.M. *Statistics in the Computer Age.* American Elsevier, 1969.

2. Macaulay, F.R. "The Smoothing of Time Series." National Bureau of Economic Research, New York, 1931.

3. Shirk, Gertrude, "Cycle Analysis—A Case Study, Part 12: A Pause for Questions," *Cycles,* Vol. XXIII, No. 5, p. 126. May 1972.

APPENDIX TO CHAPTER FIVE

Assigning Dates to Filtered Data

Figure 5-19 shows this principle, using a 7-point filter for illustration. The filter can be any length, but choosing an odd number of points for your filter simplifies date assignment; otherwise, the dates will fall between the output data points.

Assign the dates of your raw input data points to the output data points of the filter, after skipping one-half the width of the filter at the beginning, and stopping short of the end by one-half the filter width. This means that you will "lose" seven points of your raw input data with a 7-point filter.

Raw input data points: . . . .

Filter at beginning of run: . . . . Filter at end of run: . . . .

Output of filter: . . . .

FIGURE 5-19. Illustration of assigning dates to filter output, showing how data is "lost" at beginning and end of data series.

Example Values for Filters

The numbers are given here for some of the filters studied in this chapter. These are low pass filters, so they are intended to add up to one (approximately).

The trapezoidal filters for Figure 5-5 and 5-7.

A	B	C	D
0	0	0	0
.05	.005	.0032	.0025
.05	.01	.0064	.005
.05	.015	.0095	.0075
.05	.02	.0127	.01
.05	.025	.0159	.0125

.05	.03	.019	.015
.05	.035	.0222	.0175
.05	.04	.0254	.02
.05	.045	.0285	.0225
.05	.05	.0317	.025
.05	.05	.0347	.0275
.05	.05	.038	.03
.05	.05	.0412	.0325
.05	.05	.0443	.035
.05	.05	.0475	.0375
.05	.05	.0475	.04
.05	.05	.0475	.0425
.05	.05	.0475	.045
.05	.05	.0475	.0475
.05	.05	.0475	.05
0	.045	.0475	.0475
	.04	.0443	.045
	.035	.0412	.0425
	etc.	.038	.04
		etc.	etc.

Note: The numbers are grouped in fives for easy reading; the grouping has no functional significance as a filter.

Half sine wave (curve A of Figure 5-7 and 5-8); 23 points total, 19 points "effective".

0.00855356
0.01696292
0.02508389
0.03277227
0.03990352
0.04634655
0.05199648
0.05676157
0.06055660
0.06330943

0.06498080
0.06554449
0.06498080
0.06330943
0.06055660
0.05676157
0.05199648
0.04634655
0.03990352
0.03277227
0.02508389
0.01696292
0.00855356

Flat-top sine waves of Figure 5-9; 27 points and 59 points.

.0098	.00213
.0190	.00424
.0272	.00630
.0342	.00829
.0394	.01019
.0426	.01198
.0437	.01363
.0437	.01514
.0437	.01648
.0437	.01764
.0437	.01861
.0437	.01938
.0437	.01993
.0437	.02026
.0437	.02037
.0437	.02037
.0437	.02037
.0437	.02037
.0437	.02037
.0437	.02037
.0437	.02037
.0426	.02037

.0394	.02037
.0342	.02037
.0272	.02037
.0190	.02037
.0098	.02037
	.02037
	.02037
	.02037
	.02037
	.02037
	.02037
	.02037
	.02037
	.02037
	.02037
	.02037
	.02037
	.02037
	.02037
	.02037
	.02037
	.02037
	.02037
	.02026
	.01993
	.01938
	.01861
	.01764
	.01648
	.01514
	.01363
	.01198
	.01019
	.00829
	.00630
	.00424
	.00213

6
Feedback Filters

We are constantly misled by the ease with which our minds fall into the ruts of one or two experiences.
SIR WILLIAM OSLER

In a feedback filter, some of the output data is fed back to the input. Feedback filters are sometimes called *recursive.* Another name for feedback filters is infinite impulse response (IIR)—the data that was fed back keeps on circulating through the filter until it gradually dies away.

If you look long enough at a feed-forward-only low pass filter, you can more or less visualize how it smooths the data. But the action of a feedback filter is less obvious at first; it may even seem strange and mysterious. I will attempt to explain how they perform in such a way as to remove as much of the mystery as possible. Feedback filters are worthwhile to use because they simplify the computer's task.

AVERAGE

In Chapter 2 we talked about averages. That material is a good introduction to this section, so if averages are not clear in your mind you may wish to review that chapter to refresh your memory.

The average is calculated by adding all the individual numbers and dividing the total by the number of pieces of data, N. Figure 6–1(a) is a signal flow diagram for calculating the average.

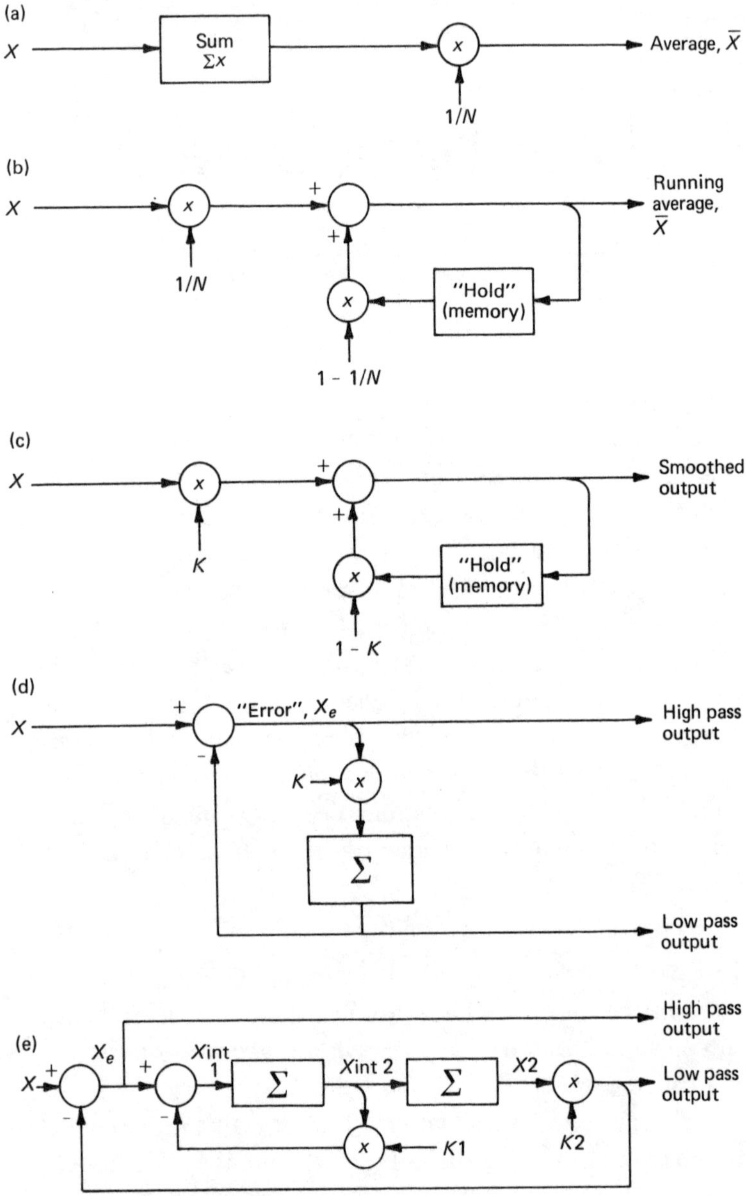

FIGURE 6-1. Signal flow diagrams for averaging and filtering. Part (e) is a second order filter.

THE RUNNING AVERAGE

It might be desirable to know, for example, the current batting average of a baseball player. This could be done by recalculating the average every day, as in the paragraphs above, but there is an easier way. The previous running average can be *updated* to incorporate the new data by adding it to the previous average after multiplying each by an appropriate factor. Figure 6–1(b) is the signal flow diagram for this updating algorithm. The resulting number for the average is the same whichever way it is calculated; but the advantage of this method is that it requires only one number to be retained in memory, not all the individual pieces of data in the entire time series.

FILTERS

The running average gives *equal weight* to all the data since the beginning of the year (Figure 6–2(a)); but that is not always what is wanted. Suppose that the interesting quantity is not the average temperature, but rather the performance of a ball player (or the market price of a security). Maybe the player's score improved with time. To estimate his present level of skill, a different kind of average is needed, one that gives more weight to *recent* data (Figure 6–2(b)). This can be achieved with only a slight change from Figure 6–1(b). All that is required is to replace the multiplying factor $1/N$ (where N is the (increasing) number of data points), by a constant, K. This is the type of "sliding" process that people usually have in mind when they speak of a *filter*. The resulting algorithm is shown in Figure 6–1(c).

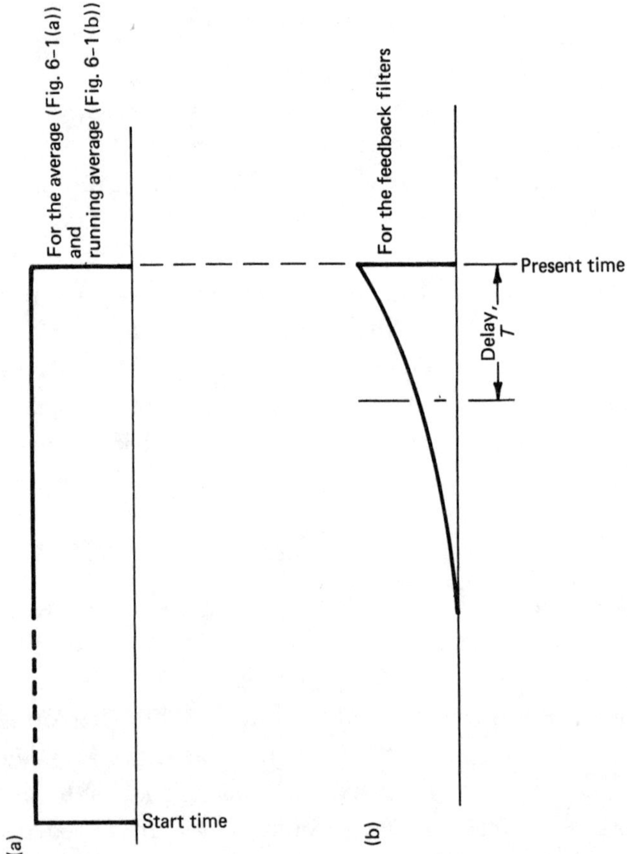

FIGURE 6-2. Memory weighting.

VISUALIZATION

While looking at Figures 6–1(b) and 6–1(c), it is natural to think of the action of a recursive filter in this way: In each of its repetitive cycles, the algorithm mixes the raw input data, X, with a fraction of the old, smoothed data. If the filter is to respond *slowly* to input changes, then the "mix" will include a lot of the old and a little of the new, and vice versa.

Figure 6–1(d) suggests a different visualization: The input is compared with the smoothed output. The difference, or "error," is accumulated from cycle to cycle of the algorithm, and this accumulated error becomes the smoothed output. Thus, if the input remains constant, the output will tend to approach it after a time as in Figure 6–4(a); and if K is increased the approach will be faster.

These images lead to the same result, but both viewpoints are useful and instructive.

The low pass output of Figure 6–1(d) is equivalent to the output of Figure 6–1(c). This equivalence is described in the appendix of this chapter. Figure 6–1(d) contains a high pass output as well as low pass.

SELECTIVITY

The ability of a filter to suppress certain kinds of fluctuations and pass others is called its frequency response, or selectivity. The selectivity of the Figure 6–1(d) filter is shown in Figure 6–3, (a) and (b).

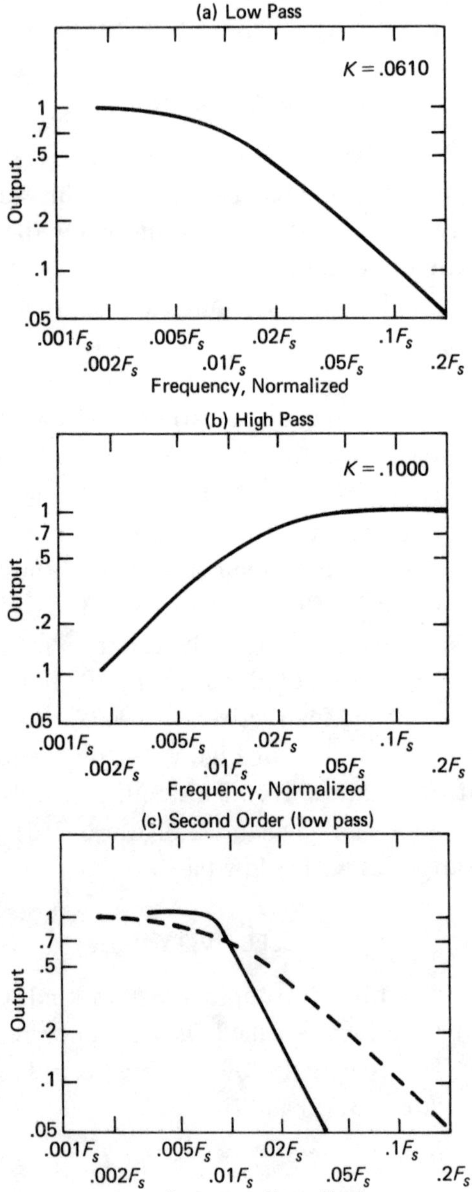

FIGURE 6-3. Frequency response.

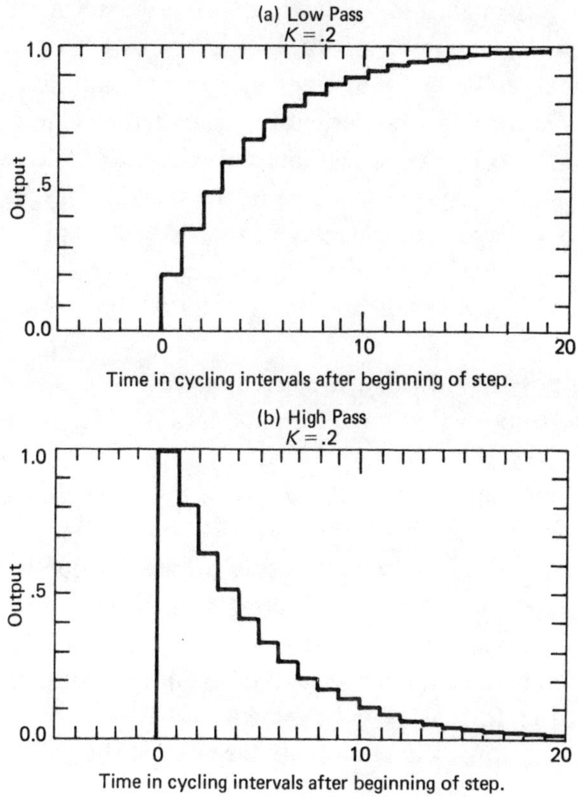

FIGURE 6-4. Time response, with unit step input.

CUTOFF FREQUENCY

The main characteristic of a filter is its cutoff frequency, also called the bandwidth in the case of a low pass filter. This section uses the traditional definition of cutoff frequency, where the overall amplification is 0.707 ($\sqrt{2}/2$).

The designer of the filter sets its cutoff frequency to the desired value by choosing the value of K. For a low cutoff frequency, K is small, and for a high cutoff frequency K is larger (but rarely greater than 1; ordinarily the cutoff frequency is lower than the sampling frequency in a digital filter).

In Figure 6–5, the dashed line shows the value to use for K. The horizontal scale represents the cutoff frequency, and this is normalized in terms of the sampling frequency. (Usually the cycling frequency of the algorithm is the same as the sampling frequency. "Frequency" is the inverse of "period," which is the time interval between samples: $F = 1/T$.)

Suppose the raw data are listed on a daily basis, and you want to smooth that data and eliminate frequencies higher than one cycle per month. To do this you would choose a cutoff frequency of $F_c = .033F_s$. This falls near the middle of the bottom scale in Figure 6–5.

Figure 6–3(a) shows the rate at which the fluctuations become attenuated by the filter as a function of their frequency. In Figure 6–3(a) the cutoff frequency is $.01F_s$. At 10 times that frequency the transmission of the filter is down to 1/10, etc.

At very low frequencies, off the edge of the chart:

$$K = 2\pi F_c / F_s.$$

Also, the time delay for a feedback filter is $1/K$ data sample intervals.

LOW PASS AND HIGH PASS FILTERS

The Figure 6–1(c) filter attenuates the high frequency fluctuations (Figure 6–3(a)), so it is called a *low pass* filter. A *high pass* filter (Figure 6–3(b)) does the opposite and at-

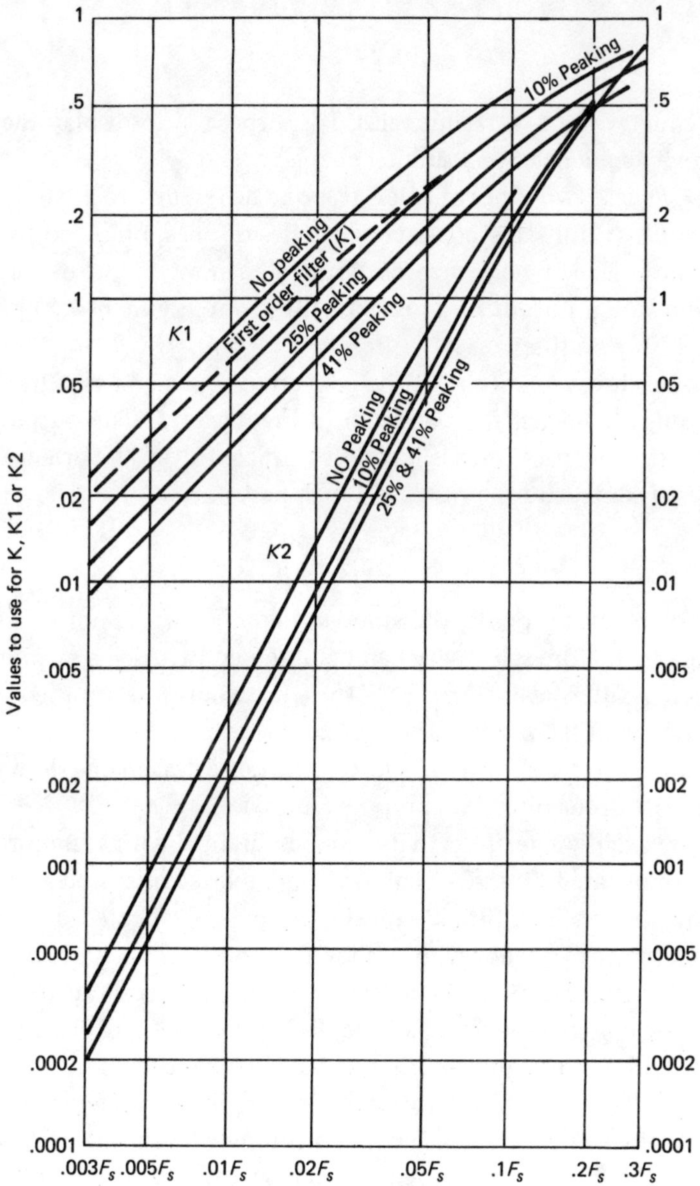

FIGURE 6-5. Values to use for K to obtain the desired bandwidth and stability.

tenuates the low frequencies. Its purpose is to display the high frequencies and sudden changes.

These two types of filters respond differently to a "step" input. A unit step consists of a series of ones, preceded for convenience by a few zeros. With a step input, Figure 6–4(a) shows the output of a low pass filter, and Figure 6–4(b) of a high pass filter.

A low pass filter can be converted to a high pass filter, using the signal flow diagram in Figure 5–13. The output of the low pass filter is merely subtracted from the original input data, and the result is a high pass output.

SECOND ORDER FILTERS

For many purposes, the slope in Figure 6–3(a) is not steep enough. More selectivity can be obtained by using a *second order* filter, as in Figure 6–1(e) (the other filters in Figure 6–1 are first order). The frequency response of a second order filter is shown in Figure 6–3(c); the dashed line shows a first order filter for comparison.

Even greater selectivity can be obtained with still more complicated filters. Telephone and television systems use highly selective filters requiring more sophisticated design methods. A reader who desires to experiment with highly selective filters can find design methods among the texts in the bibliography. The LaPlace, Fourier and z transforms are useful for this purpose, but a word of caution is in order here. The great selectivity available in such filters is tempting, but they tend to "ring," and that complicates the interpretation of the data. It can even mislead a researcher into thinking he has found an oscillation in the data, when it was really generated by his filter.

However, there *is* a safe way to scan your data with great frequency selectivity, and that is to use the Fourier transform (Chapter 9). The "Fast" Fourier transform takes less computer time. Software is widely available.

DESIGNING FEEDBACK FILTERS

The Running Average

In FORTRAN or BASIC, the averaging operation shown in Figure 6–1(b) can be written:

```
Avg = X/N + (1 - 1/N)*Avg
repeat
```

where Avg is the averaged output of the algorithm,
X is the raw input data,
N is the current total number of data points (*N* increments by 1 upon each cycle of the algorithm),
and * means multiply.

Avg to the left of the = sign is the new average value, while Avg on the right is the old value obtained in the previous calculation cycle. "Repeat" is not a machine command; normally this algorithm would be part of a DO loop in FORTRAN, or a FOR . . NEXT loop in BASIC.

First Order Filter

Two different algorithms are offered, corresponding to the two viewpoints discussed previously:

FIGURE 6–1(c):

```
LPOUT = K*X + (1 - K)*LPOUT
repeat
```

The analogy is evident between this algorithm and the one above for the running average.

FIGURE 6-1(d):

HPOUT = X − LPOUT
LPOUT = LPOUT + K * HPOUT
repeat

The second line is read as: "Replace the old value for LPOUT (from the previous calculation cycle) by a new value which consists of its old value plus K times HPOUT." This is a summation process.

Both these algorithms give the same low pass output, but the second algorithm has a high pass output as well, HPOUT.

Figure 6-6 is the (program control) flow chart, and Figure 6-7 is a computer program.

Second Order Filter

A signal flow diagram for the second order filter is shown in Figure 6-1(e), and an algorithm is:

HPOUT = X − LPOUT
Xint1 = HPOUT − K1 * Xint2
Xint2 = Xint2 + Xint1
X2 = X2 + Xint2
LPOUT = K2 * X2

repeat

This flow diagram and algorithm are not unique. There are many different ways of describing and programming a second order filter.

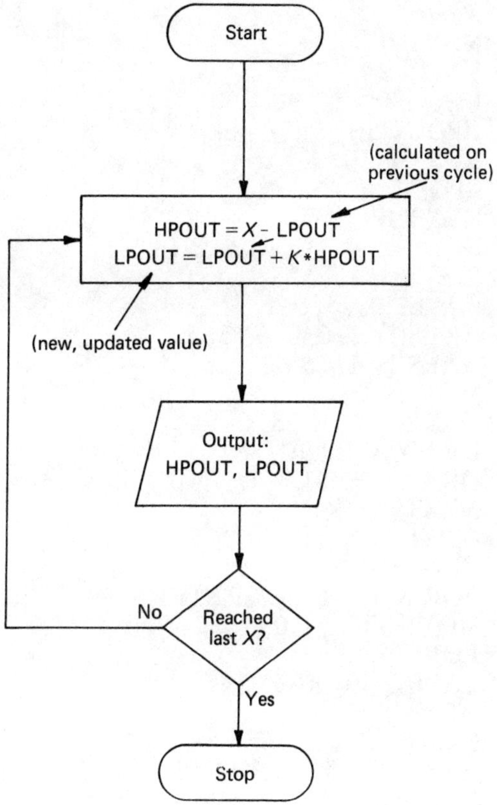

FIGURE 6-6. Flow chart for the first order filter of figure 1D.

```
10   K = .2
20   DIM X(30), HPOUT(30), LPOUT(30)
30   FOR J = 5 TO 30
40   X(J) = 1
50   NEXT J
60   S = O
70   FOR Jj = 1 TO 30
80   HPOUT(Jj) = X(Jj) - S
90   S = S + E(Jj) ÷ K
100  LPOUT(Jj) = S
110  NEXT Jj
120                   GRAPHICS
130  LOCATE 15, 115, 15, 70
140  SCALE 0, 25, 0, 1
150  AXES 1, .1, 0, 0, 5, .5, 5
160  AXES 1, .1, 25, 1, 5, .5, 5
170  MOVE 7,0
180  FOR N = 1 TO 25
190  DRAW N, LPOUT(N)
200  DRAW N + 1, LPOUT(N)
210  NEXT N
220  CSIZE 3
230  FIXED 0
240  FOR Xpos = 9 TO 29 STEP 5
250  MOVE Xpos, -.03
260  LORG 6
270  LABEL (Xpos - 9)/5
280  NEXT Xpos
290  MOVE 15, -.1
300  LABEL "TIME, IN TIME CONSTANTS (τ)"
310  FIXED 1
320  LORG 8
330  FOR Ypos = 0 TO 1 STEP .5
340  MOVE 7, Ypos
350  LABEL Ypos
360  NEXT Ypos
370  MOVE 6, .75
380  LABEL "OUTPUT"
```

```
390   PAUSE
400   DUMP GRAPHICS
410   GCLEAR
420   STOP
430   END
```

FIGURE 6-7. Program for Figure 6-1(d). (H-P BASIC)

A second order filter can generate an oscillation; this is usually undesirable. A way to avoid oscillations is to set the constants $K1$ and $K2$ to the values shown in Figure 6–5 (solid lines). The upper family of lines is for $K1$, and the lower family (sloping more steeply) is for $K2$.

In designing a second order filter you must decide on the amount of *relative stability* you want. In Figure 6–8 this relative stability is described in terms of *peaking*. Peaking is a property of filters whereby they *amplify* certain frequencies. In this filter the amplification "peaks" (or is maximized) at about half the cutoff frequency.

You might decide that you want *no* peaking, just true values. Figure 6–5 contains a pair of lines for zero peaking, but zero peaking filters are not very popular. The other filters are more selective (Figure 6–8), and a little peaking is usually not troublesome. The lines show peaking values up to 41%. You may experiment with even greater peaking if you wish, but your filter will then begin to "ring" (Figure 6–9).

Figure 6–5 (solid lines) shows the values to use for $K1$ and $K2$ to achieve the desired cutoff frequency.

With sampled data, it is not very useful for the cutoff frequency to approach one-half the sampling frequency so Figure 6–5 stops before then. At the other extreme the lines

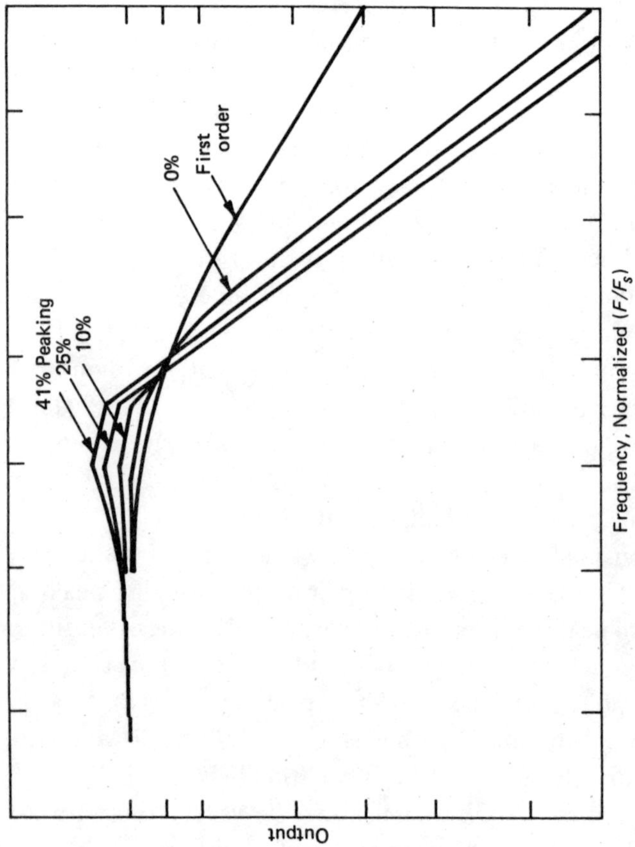

FIGURE 6-8. In a second order filter, greater selectivity is obtained by accepting greater "peaking".

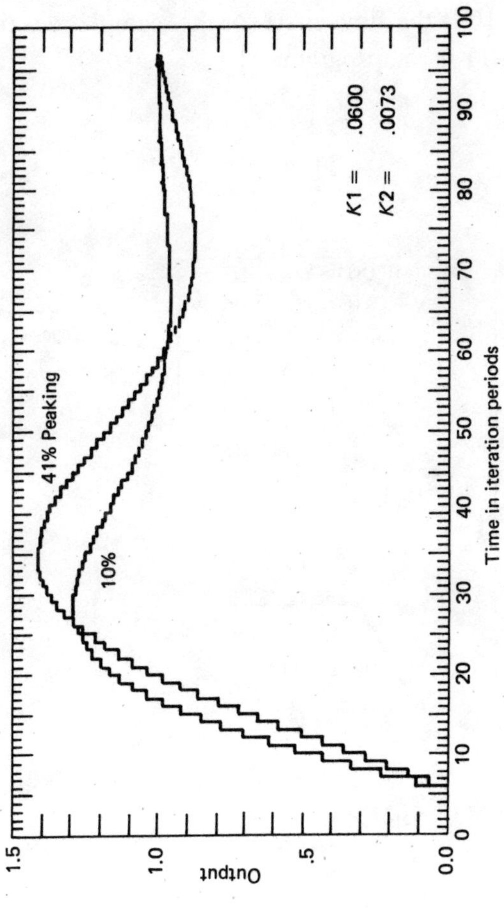

FIGURE 6-9. Time response of second order filter with step input. With increased peaking, the filter begins to ring.

become straight. To design a filter that is off the chart, extrapolate $K1$ in proportion to the cutoff frequency, and $K2$ in proportion to the square of the cutoff frequency.

Figure 6–10 is the flow chart for the second order filter, and Figure 6–11 is the program.

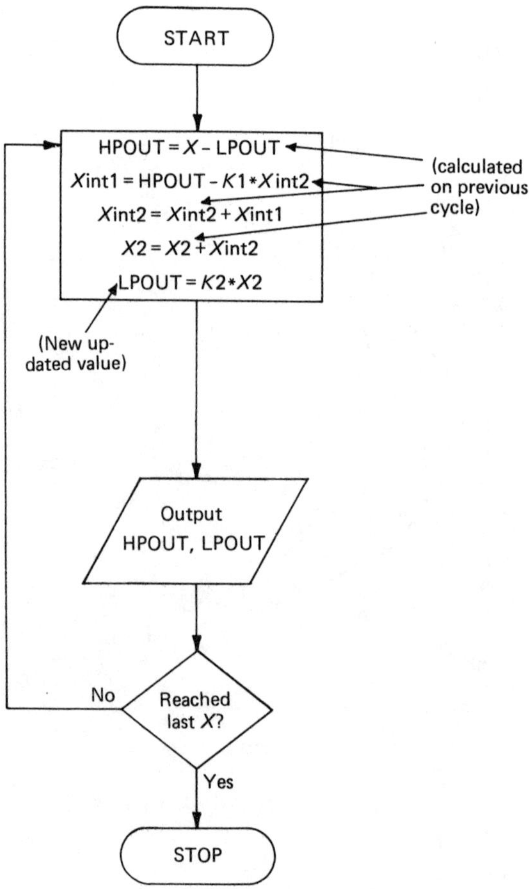

FIGURE 6-10. Flowchart for the second order filter of Figure 6-1(e).

```
10
20
30      THIS ONE IS SECOND ORDER LOW PASS
40
50      FIXED 4
60      PRINT "  "
70      PRINT "  "
80      PRINT "Type in the value of K1"
90      INPUT K1
100     PRINT K1
110     PRINT "Type in the value of K2"
120     INPUT K2
130     PRINT K2
140     DIM X(100), Hpout(100), Lpout(100)
150
160     FOR J = 5 TO 100
170     X(J)=1
180     NEXT J
190     PRINT "  "
200
210     FOR Ji = 2 TO 100
220     Hpout(Jj) = X(Jj) - Lpout(Jj - 1)
230     Xint1 = Hpout(Jj) - K1 * Xint2
240     Xint2 = Xint2 + Xint1
250     X2 = X2 + Xint
260     Lpout(Jj) = K2 * X2
270     NEXT Jj
280
290
300                 GRAPHICS
310
320     LOCATE 15, 115, 15, 70
330     SCALE 0, 100, 0, 1.5
340     FIXES 1, .1, 0, 0, 5, .5, 5
350     FIXES 1, .1, 100, 1.5, 5, .5, 5
360     MOVE 7,0
370     FOR N = 1 TO 100
380     DRAW N, Lpout(N)
390     DRAW N + 1, Lpout(N)
```

```
400 NEXT N
410 CSIZE 3
420 FIXED 0
430 FOR Xpos = 14.5 TO 114.5 STEP 10
440 MOVE Xpos, -.04
450 LORG 6
460 LABEL Xpos - 14.5
470 NEXT Xpos
480 MOVE 62, -.12
490 LABEL "TIME, IN ITERATION PERIODS"
500 LORG 8
510 FIXED 1
520 FOR Xpos = 0 TO 1.5 STEP .5
530 MOVE 27.5, Ypos
540 LABEL Ypos
550 NEXT Ypos
560 MOVE 22, .75
570 LABEL "OUTPUT"
580 FIXED 4
590 MOVE 121, .24
600 LABEL "                K1 = ", K1
610 MOVE 121, .13
620 LABEL "                K2 = ", K2
630 PAUSE
640 DUMP GRAPHICS
650 GCLEAR
660 STOP
670 END
```

FIGURE 6-11. Filter program, second order. (H-P BASIC)

APPENDIX TO CHAPTER SIX

Equivalence of Figures 6–1(c) and 6–1(d)

In Figure 6-12(a) the low pass filter is shown in abbreviated form by a single block. In Figure 6-12(b), the complete filter is drawn as it was in Figure 6-1(c); otherwise 6-12(a) and (b) are the same.

Inside Figure 6-12(b) there is an internal feedback loop having the multiplying factor "1 - *K*." Block diagrams can be manipulated with certain restrictions, and the rules[1] permit separating the "1" and the "*K*" into two separate loops; this is shown in Figure 6-12(c). Then in Figure 6-12(d) the "*K*" feedback loop has been shifted to utilize the other "*K*" multiplier; one "*K*" now serves both functions. In Figure 6-12(e) two changes are made: (1) two subtraction operations are combined into one, and (2) the delay and the "+1" feedback loop have been replaced by a summation block, to simplify the sketch. These two operations are mathematically equivalent, as shown in Figure 6-13.

The final result of this conversion, Figure 6-12(e), is repeated on the summary chart as Figure 6-1(d) which contains a high pass output as well as the low pass output of Figure 6-1(c).

REFERENCE TO APPENDIX

1. Mason, S.J., and Zimmermann, H.J., "Electronic Circuits," *Signals and Systems,* Wiley, 1960.

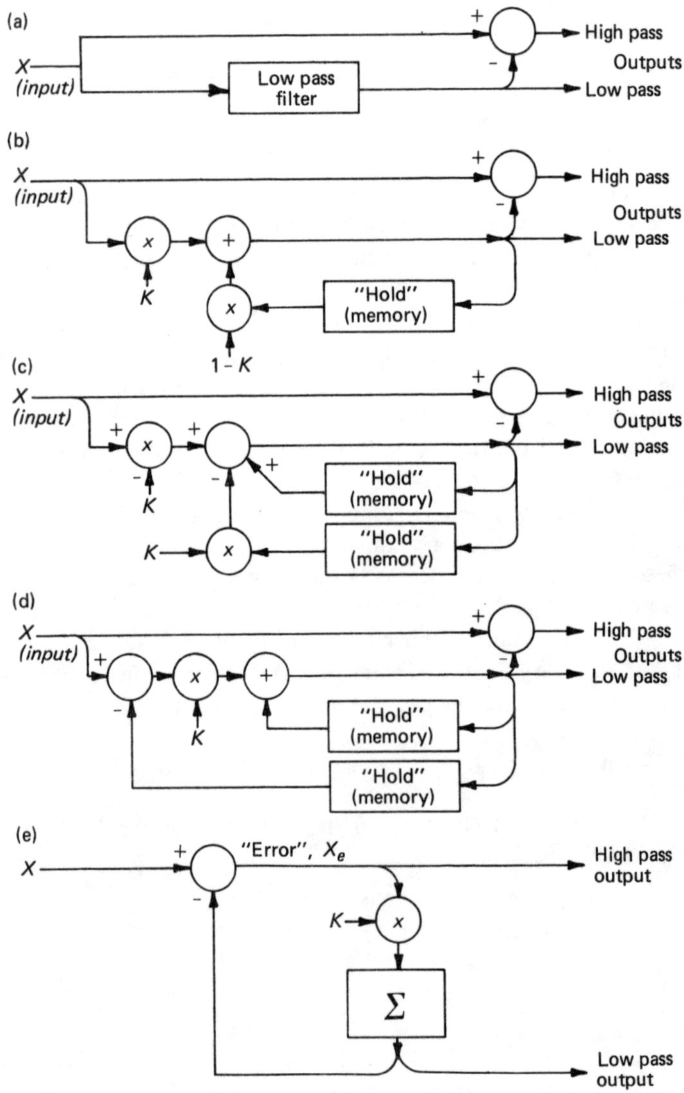

FIGURE 6-12. Equivalence of Figure 6-1(c) with 6-1(d).

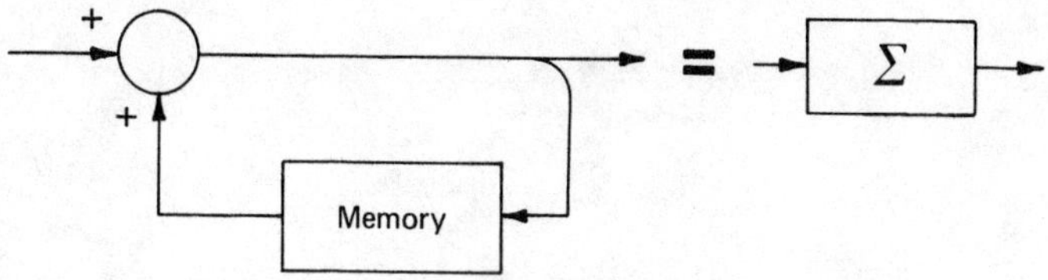

FIGURE 6-13. Positive feedback with unity gain performs summation.

7
Stock Price Oscillations

If we could find a steady oscillation in the data, we could use it to buy low and sell high. An attempt was made to find a useful oscillation in the overall market for common stocks by using a filter. The effective span of the filter was 19 weeks, and the numbers used in it are shown in the appendix for Chapter 5. Each raw input data point represents one week, and is the average of the closing prices for each day of that week.

In Figure 7-1—repeated here for further examination—the upper plot contains the low frequencies, i.e. those having a period longer than 19 weeks. The higher frequencies are in Figure 7-2, shown expanded for easy study.

The most striking feature of Figure 7-1 is the market break in 1929, followed by the great skid into the depression which bottomed-out in 1932. This crash is also evident in the high frequency data of Figure 7-2.

Another feature of Figure 7-1 is that the "even" values of the Dow seemed to possess a magic of their own. Dow 100 acted as a resistance level from 1915 to 1924, and again in 1933 and 1934. It then acted as a support level in 1941 after the bombing of Pearl Harbor. Then, in 1966, the Dow

FIGURE 7-1. Stock price index after filtering (low pass).

reached 1,000, and that number acted as a resistance level until 1982.

Of course, these resistance and support levels are purely psychological. The *real* market value of blue chip stocks (upon which the Dow is based) has suffered drastically since 1966 because of inflation. This is shown in Figure 2–3 of Chapter 2. The market is very depressed, and we will find out in the next few years how much of that loss is permanent and how much can be recovered. If much of it is recoverable, we may have a great bull market ahead.

Figures 7–2(a), (b) and (c) were plotted in the hope of finding a quicker cycle than the business cycle, which is about 4 years, more or less. Clearly we might be able to make money faster on a high frequency cycle than on a low one. There is indeed some action in some parts of Figure 7–2. Sometimes there is an oscillation with a period of about 3 to 5 months[3], but it is usually barely enough to pay the commission on a small trade. Keep it in mind, though, especially if you are a member of a stock exchange so that you do not have to pay a commission. It may be that more volatile ("high Beta"*) stocks react to it more than is implied by Figure 7–2.

Proceeding to the next range of frequencies, we look for oscillations having periods up to 4 years long. Figure 7–3 is the low pass output of a 4-year filter which will be de-

---

*The Beta value for a stock is a measure of its volatility. Some stocks are more volatile than the average, that is, they tend to rise and fall more than the average. For example, a Beta value of 1.5 would describe a stock that tends to rise and fall 1.5 times as much (in percentage) as the average of many stocks.

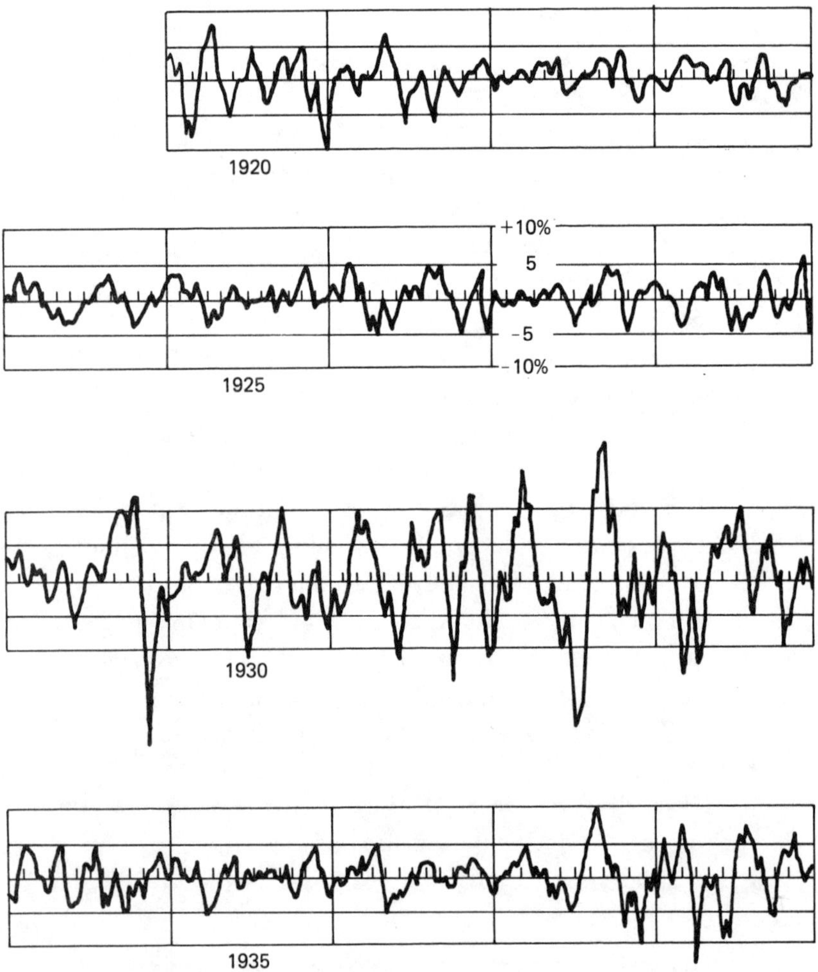

FIGURE 7-2(a). The high frequencies removed from Figure 1 and spread out for analysis.

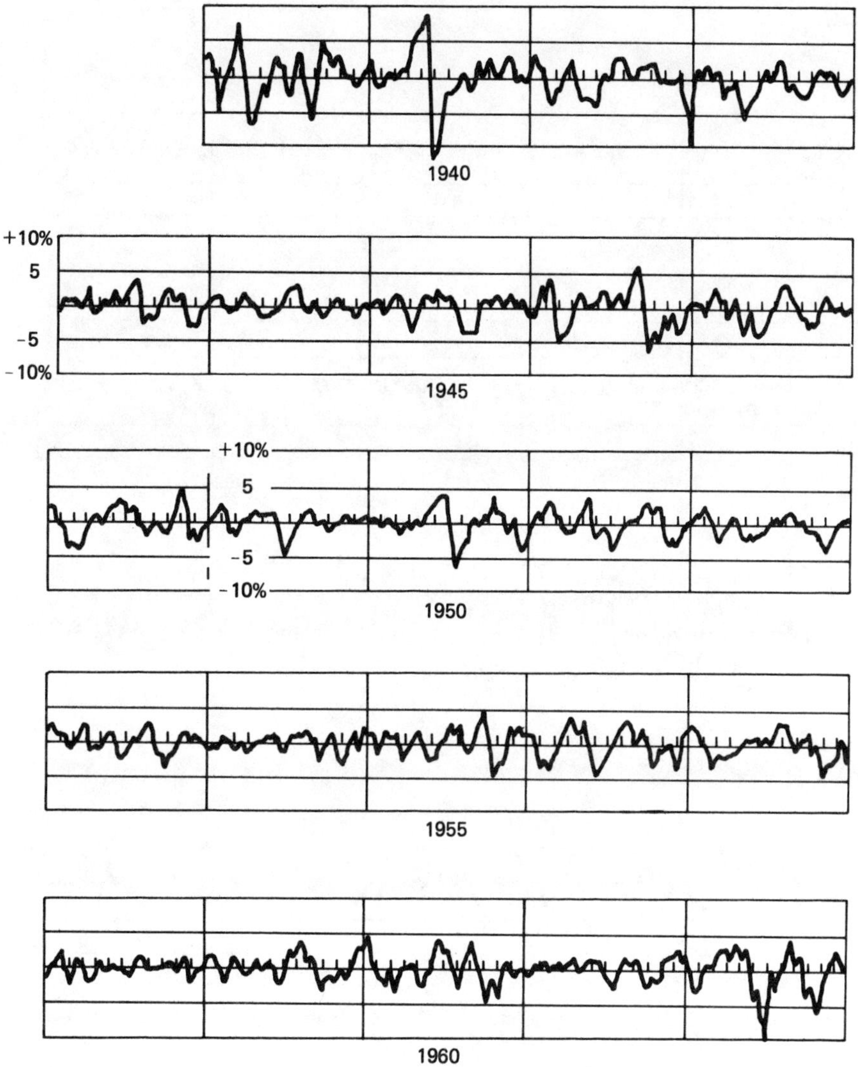

FIGURE 7-2(b). The high frequencies removed from Figure 1 and spread out for analysis.

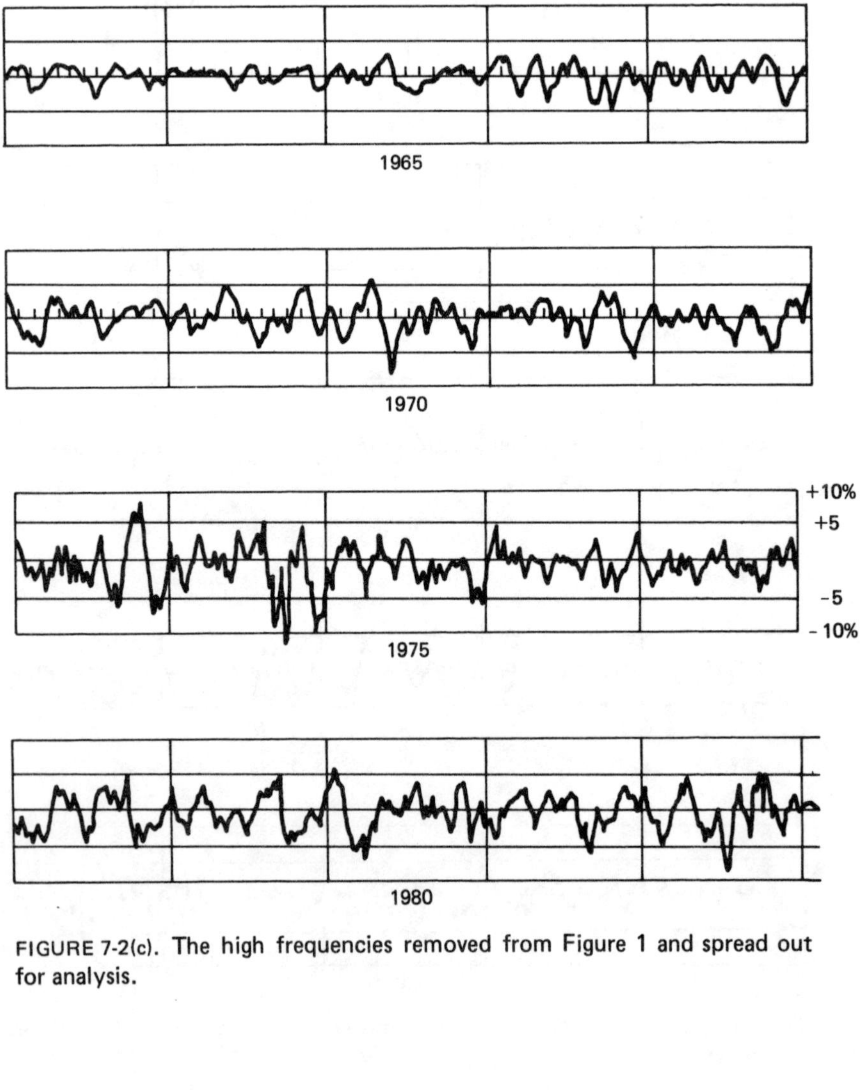

FIGURE 7-2(c). The high frequencies removed from Figure 1 and spread out for analysis.

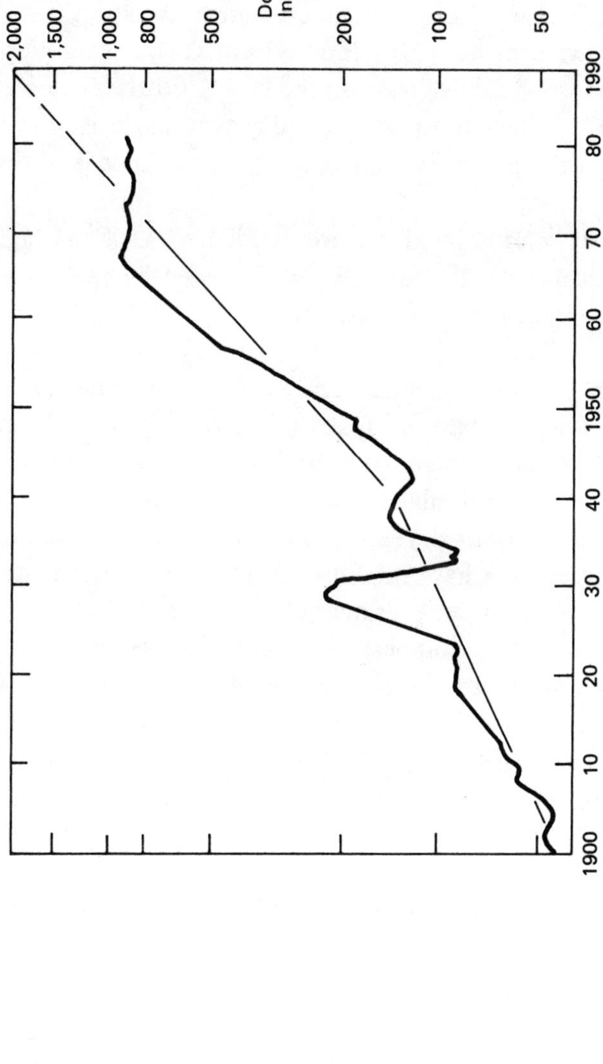

FIGURE 7-3. Trend and low frequencies of the Dow Jones Industrials Index, after smoothing-out the 4-year and shorter fluctuations.

scribed later. It shows a general trend upward, and the trend became steeper since the onset of inflation in the 1930's. The lines show an average slope of 5.5% per year since then, and 3% before. (These lines were drawn by estimation.)

If the straight line is projected ahead to the year 1990, it reaches Dow 2,000 by then. Of course, the straight lines were drawn arbitrarily, but it does look like the market that was "snagged" for 16 years on the Dow 1,000 level now has a lot of catching up to do. Some day that magic 1,000 will turn into a support level instead of the resistance level that it has been.

Another prominent feature of Figure 7-3 is the rapid price advance of the late 1920's, followed by the violent contraction of the early 1930's.

Aside from these two features–the great boom and depression and the emotional barriers at Dow 100 and 1,000–the fluctuations have been stripped from Figure 7-3, and we expect to find them in the high pass output, Figure 7-4. Here, the most prominent feature is a nearly regular oscillation about every 4 years. Some writers call this the political cycle, so I have re-plotted it (tracing by hand) on a repeated scale of the presidential term cycle in Figure 7-5. There certainly does appear to be a correlation between election times and stock prices. Originally, some investors ascribed this correlation to the Federal Reserve Board and their control of the money supply; but I extended the plot backward before 1914 (the Board's year of initiation), and this correlation was already in existence (Figure 7-6).

These swings are large enough to use for speculation. Even if you are not a speculator but an investor, you should

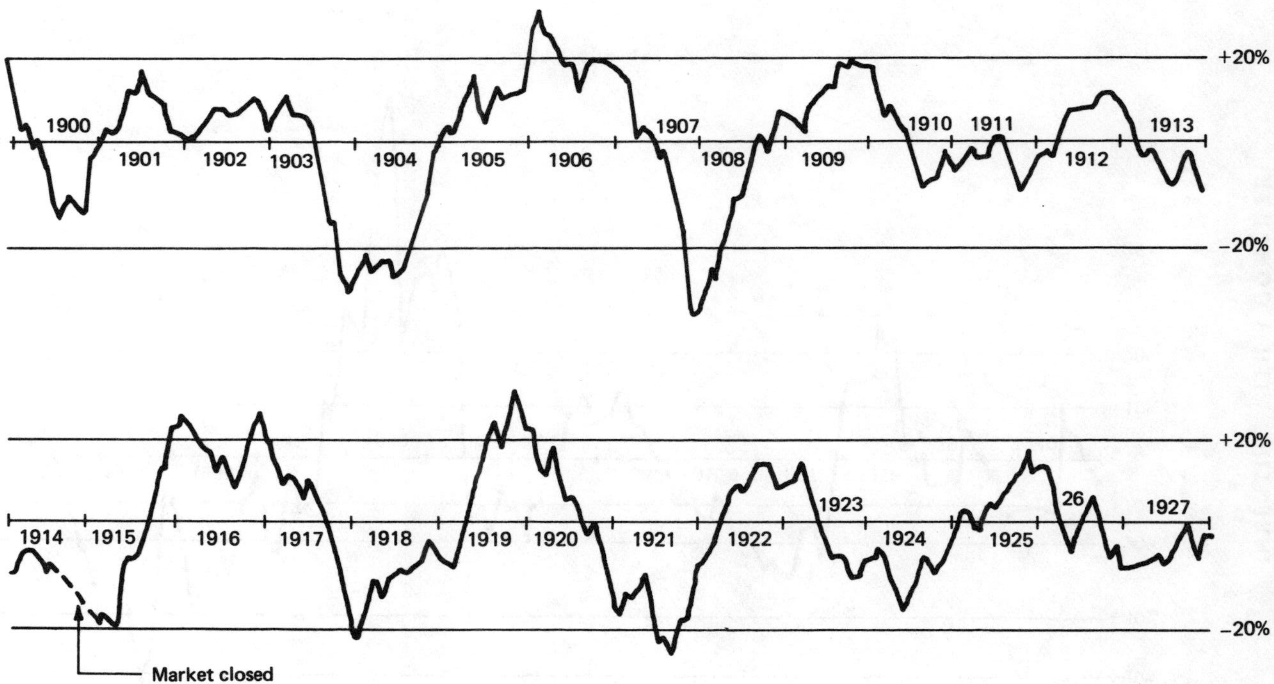

FIGURE 7-4(a). The Dow Jones Industrials after removal of low frequencies.

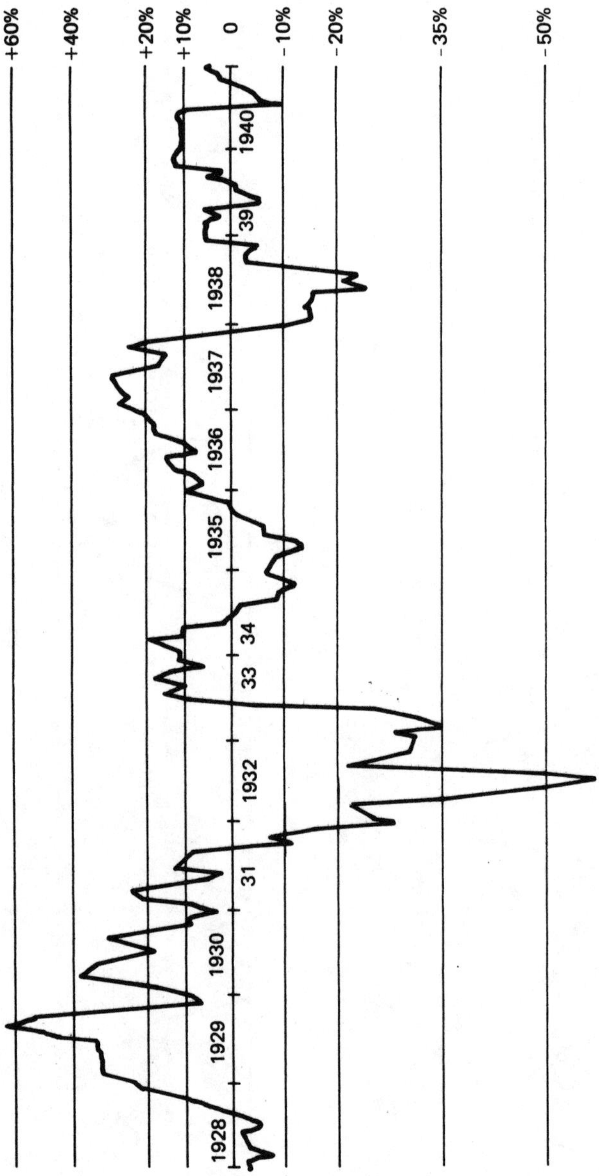
+60%
+40%
+20%
+10%
0
-10%
-20%
-35%
-50%
1928
1929
1930
31
1932
33
34
1935
1936
1937
1938
39
1940

FIGURE 7-4(b).

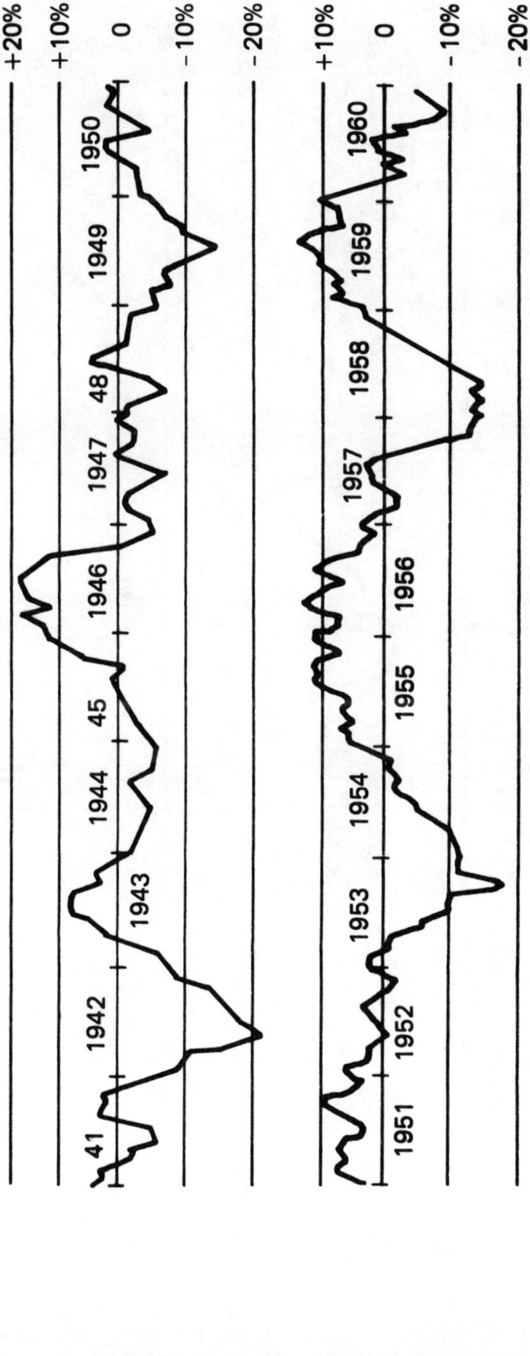
+20%
+10%
0
-10%
-20%
41
1942
1943
1944
45
1946
1947
48
1949
1950
+10%
0
-10%
-20%
1951
1952
1953
1954
1955
1956
1957
1958
1959
1960

FIGURE 7-4(c).

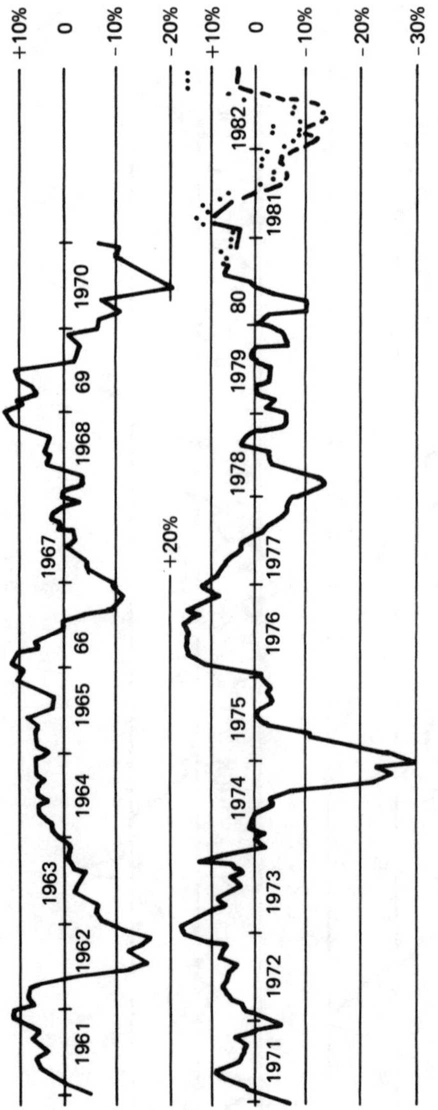
+10%
0
-10%
-20%
+20%
+10%
0
-10%
-20%
-30%
1961
1962
1963
1964
1965
66
1967
1968
69
1970
1971
1972
1973
1974
1975
1976
1977
1978
1979
80
1981
1982

FIGURE 7-4(d).

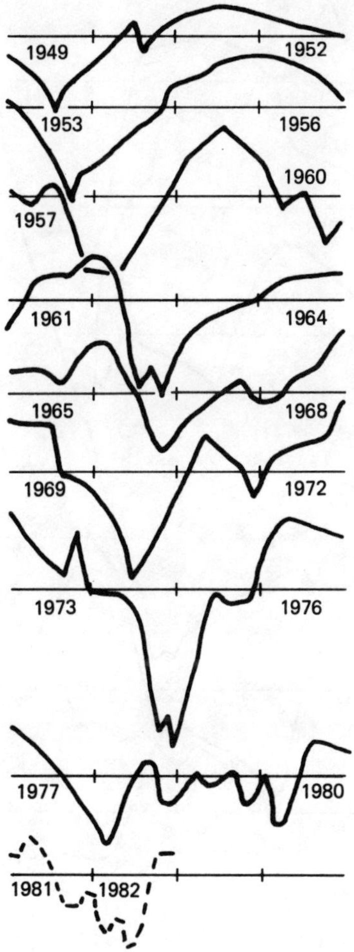

FIGURE 7-5. The plots of Figure 7-4, arrayed by the presidential election cycle (4 years).

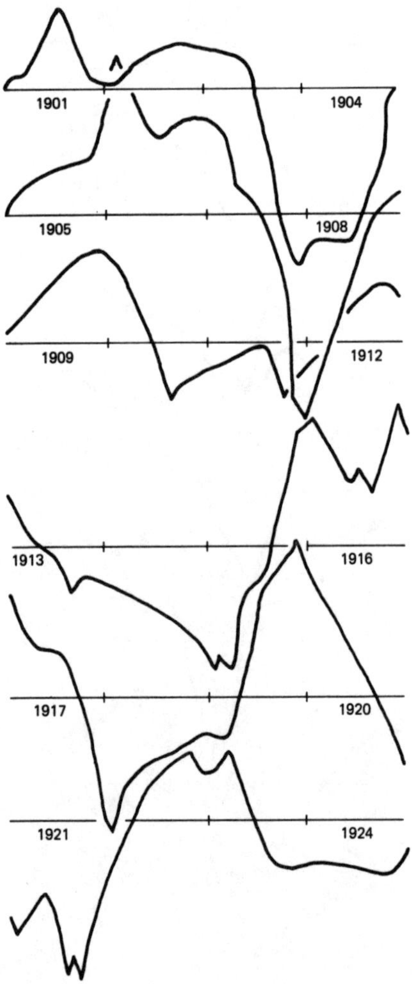

FIGURE 7-6. The same as in 7-5 except before 1925.

take them into account when timing your purchases and sales. I feel that everyone should try very hard to understand the business cycle and to predict what it will do next.

If you have a data base for individual stocks or commodities, you can apply filtering to them too. Hurst[1] recommended that we always look for an oscillation in the price of a security in the hope that it will continue for at least one more swing. This is worth considering.

The data for the plots in this chapter were obtained by filtering from a raw data base of the Dow Jones Industrial Index from 1897 to 1982. The data are weekly and represent the close of the market, except that the early data points represent the average of the daily closing prices. This data base happens to be in logarithm form (see Chapter 10).

It was desired to limit the size of the filter used, so for the four-year filter that produced Figures 7–3 and 7–4, the weekly data were first passed through a low pass filter consisting of the following numbers:

0.125
0.25
0.25
0.25
0.125

In effect, this converted the data to monthly data (approximately). These smoothed data were then refiltered with the 59-point filter, and both the high pass and low pass outputs were used. The filter and the program are included in Chapter 5 in the Appendix. The effect of the 59-point filter in this case was to segregate the oscillations having a period of about 4 years and shorter in the high pass output, while the general trend and the slow oscillations were contained in the low pass output.

In Figures 7–4 and 7–5, the data for 1981 and 1982 are dashed. In effect, these are predictions. Recall that a 4-year filter "loses" the first and last 2 years of data because of its symmetry. In Figure 7–4(d), the dotted line was an attempt to extrapolate over that 2-year-period by continuing the final data point, repeating its constant value for an extra two years. The dashed line was obtained in a similar way, but assuming an uptrend in this final value. It will be interesting to see how accurate these predictions turn out to be.

REFERENCES

1. Hurst, J.M., *The Profit Magic of Stock Transaction Timing*, Prentice-Hall, 1970.
2. Klein, Roger, and Wolman, William, *The Beat Inflation Strategy*, Simon & Schuster, 1975.
3. Wilson, Louise L., "Catalogue of Cycles, Part I," *Economics*, Foundation for the Study of Cycles, 1964.

8
Generation of Oscillations

All business proceeds on beliefs, or judgements of probabilities, and not on certainties.
CHARLES WILLIAM ELLIOT

This chapter and the next are closely related. In this chapter we wonder what social or economic processes could generate oscillations in the price of a security, and we try to gain some insight into this by looking at physical processes from an engineering viewpoint. In the following chapter we conjecture about the frequency spectra that should be generated by such oscillations, and whether it might be possible to identify the type of oscillation by studying its spectrum. These chapters are based on sound engineering principles, but talking about a single method of generation in isolation is necessarily an idealized concept; and whether the methods of Chapter 9 would actually work in the real world where data are corrupted by "noise" is highly speculative.

But it *is* worth discussing. It seems important to me to examine how well our economic institutions perform their assigned tasks, and this kind of approach has been neglected in the past.

When we do discover an oscillation in our financial data, we need to know some things before we can make intelligent guesses about what might have caused it. Key parameters are:

1. How precise is its timing?
2. How long will it last?

To begin with, we will expect to find two different kinds of oscillations:

1. Precisely regular, "clock-controlled" oscillations, and
2. Oscillations that are irregular in frequency.

We will also expect to find oscillations derived from either of the above sources, but which have been greatly changed by other circumstances, so that they are even more irregular in amplitude and phase. These modifications will be discussed more in the following chapter.

PRECISE FREQUENCY OSCILLATIONS

Two sources of precisely regular oscillations are:

1. Astronomical events, and
2. Calendar events.

Examples of astronomical events are:

1. The variation of light and temperature throughout the day;
2. The variation of the weather throughout the year; and
3. The tide as controlled by the moon.

Figures 8–1(a) and (b) show the annual cycle in construction activity as it varies under the influence of (mostly, presumably) the weather.

The lunar tide is another example of an oscillation that is precisely controlled in frequency but whose effects are strongly modified by location on the earth and by the local undersea topography. Sea traffic has been economically important for millenia, and so tidal currents and the threat of running aground are very important to a ship's captain. These problems are solved by tide tables which can be calculated and printed years in advance because of the regularity of the earth's rotation and of the moon's position. But in their use, both the phase and amplitude of the tide must be corrected for location. The height of the tide varies from less than 0.5 meter to more than 10 meters at various locations.

(a).

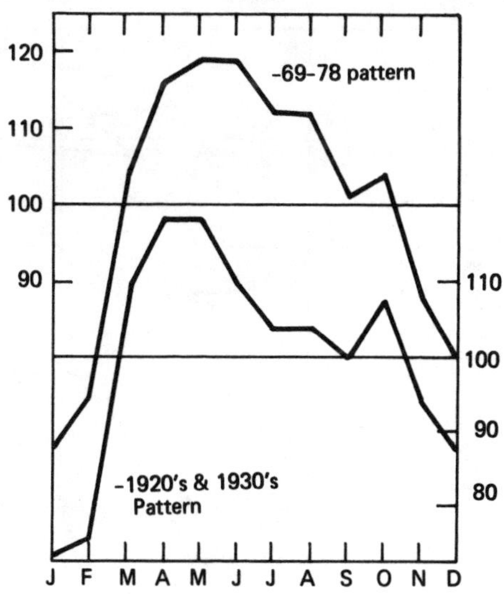

FIGURE 8-1

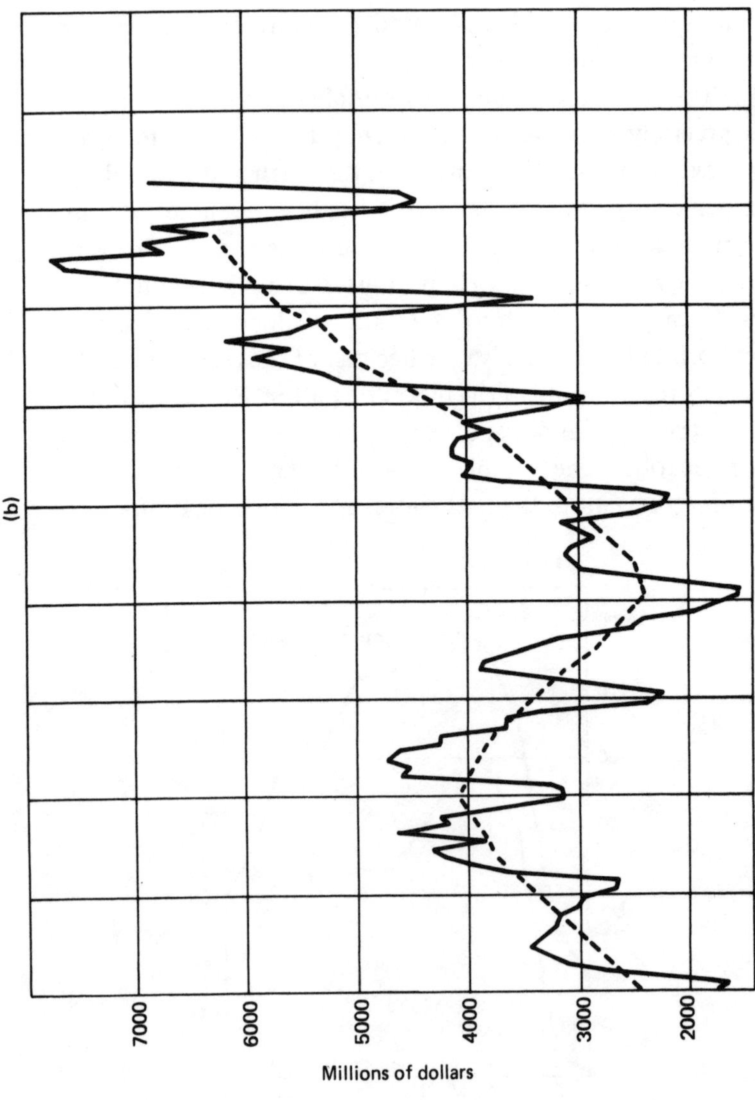

FIGURE 8-1. The monthly value of residential construction contracts. Copyright 1979 by Foundation for the Study of Cycles, 124 S. Highland Ave., Pittsburgh, PA 15206 (by permission).

The key lesson here is that the actual tide is too "noisy" (because of local water and wind effects) to extrapolate for years ahead but the basic astronomical cause is predictable for centuries in the future if required.

A possible example of a *calendar* event oscillation is the four-year political cycle (in the United States) and its alleged effect on the financial markets.

IRREGULAR OSCILLATIONS

One of the government's favorite games is *regulation* especially of financial matters; and corporations, and even people, often try to regulate their affairs too. However, regulating systems often generate oscillations, and the remainder of this chapter will investigate these.

"On-off" Regulators

Your home contains several on-off thermostats. They control your furnace and air conditioner, refrigerator, oven, water heater, and electric iron. In economics, a governing board which meets and acts only occasionally exerts on-off, "all-or-nothing" control. Interest rates, and the margin required for stock purchases stay constant for a while, then change suddenly.

On-off regulators exert their control by oscillating continually; however, the frequency varies in response to changes in the environment as shown in Figure 8–2, so I have included them in this section on "irregular" oscillations.

Resonance and Ringing in Controlled Systems

On-off is not the only kind of control; there can also be gradual, or "proportional" control. An example is steering

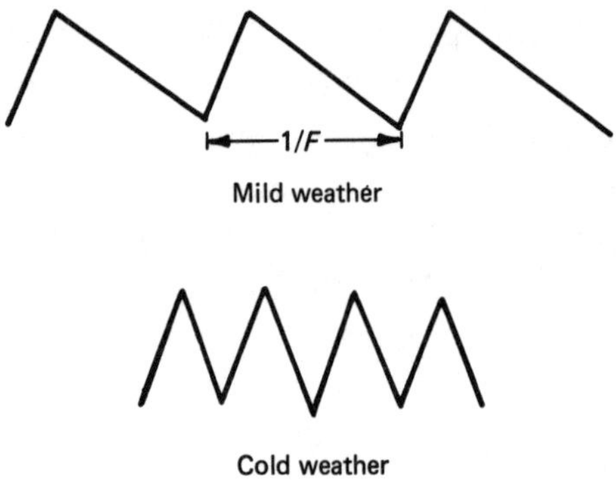

FIGURE 8-2. Variation of temperature with time with an on-off thermostat.

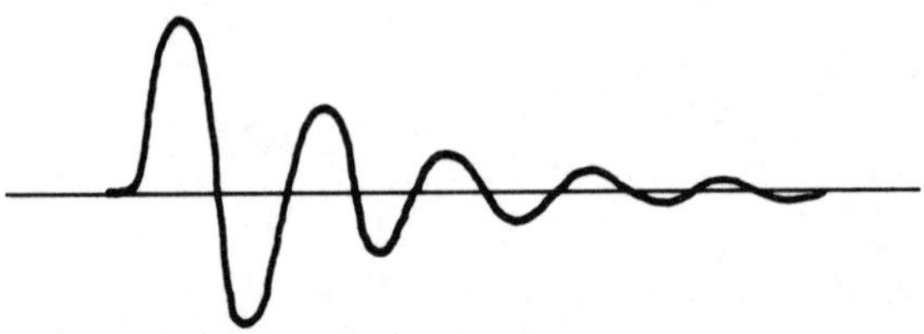

FIGURE 8-3. Ringing of a resonant system after a disturbance.

your automobile in order to stay on the road. You use *negative feedback* to steer–if the car is too far toward the right-hand side of the road, you steer toward the left, and vice versa.

In Chapter 6, I said that a feedback filter can oscillate (ring) if the wrong values are used for the multiplying constants. The same theory controls the response of a proportional regulating system, and it can "ring" too if the responses are not adjusted properly (Figure 8–3). A frequent cause of oscillation is too much time-lag in the measuring system or feedback loop.

Oscillations of irregular frequency and ringing probably have less predictive value than steady oscillations of constant frequency, but they may still be useful to a speculator.

9
Frequency Spectra

In the earlier chapters it was stated that a regular oscillation can be described in a very simple way, that is, by its frequency or period—one is the reciprocal of the other. Filters were described which could separate some frequencies from others, so that an oscillation of a certain frequency (such as the four-year cycle, for example) could be isolated from other fluctuations for individual study.

We come now to another elegant software tool, the Fourier transform. The Fourier transform can display *all* the frequencies that may be present, in a single plot. One advantage of such a display is that it can be used for making a general search for oscillations. How successfully this "prospecting" can be carried out depends on the nature of the data, and also on how good we are at suppressing the general noise background in the data. Some examples will be shown shortly.

Another reason for looking at frequency spectra is that it can help to identify the *type* of oscillation, which can lead to an identification of its *source* as discussed in Chapter 8.

The Fourier transform is neither better nor worse than the filters described in Chapters 5 and 6. The two methods are most powerful when they are regarded as complementary to each other and used together.

There is a large body of mathematical theory concerning oscillations and frequency spectra, and the reader who wishes to pursue it can check the references. Fortunately though, the principles can also be explained and understood without advanced mathematics.

We begin with what is probably the simplest of spectra, that of a continuous oscillation of constant amplitude and of precisely constant frequency. To find a practical example of such a pure oscillation requires some groping. Let me offer the rotation of the earth relative to the fixed stars; astronomers call it sidereal time. Mathematics shows that the spectrum for such a pure oscillation is simply a vertical line, as shown in Figure 9-1(a).

EFFECT OF DATA DURATION

But we will not find many such pure "lines" in the Fourier transforms of our financial data because they will be *modulated.* A simple form of modulation is caused by the *finite duration* of our data base. The spectrum for a pure oscillation of finite duration is shown in Figure 9-1(b). Since the duration of our data series is always limited, we will never expect to find a spectral "line" as in 9-1(a); the sharpest, narrowest peak that we can expect to find in a Fourier transform will have a width of $1/T$, where T is the time duration of our data series. We will expect to find some broader peaks, but none narrower than $1/T$.

This principle can be seen in the actual data. In Figure 9-2, the plot at the top was calculated from the entire 34-year span of time since 1948, at which date the effects of World War II had presumably disappeared. The effect can be seen best in the peak marked "4 years" (the 4-year cycle described in Chapter 7). The middle and bottom plots were

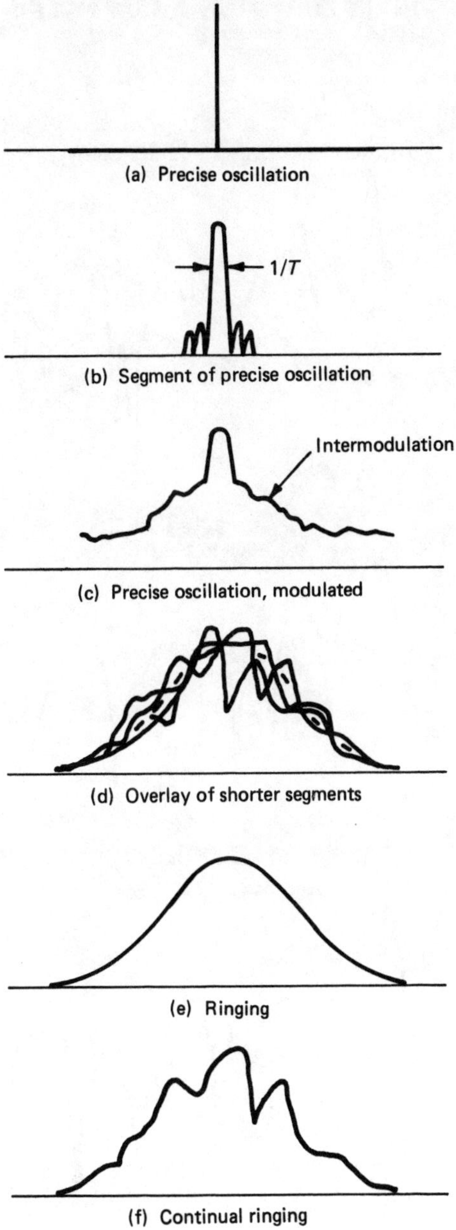

FIGURE 9-1. Frequency spectra for different kinds of oscillation.

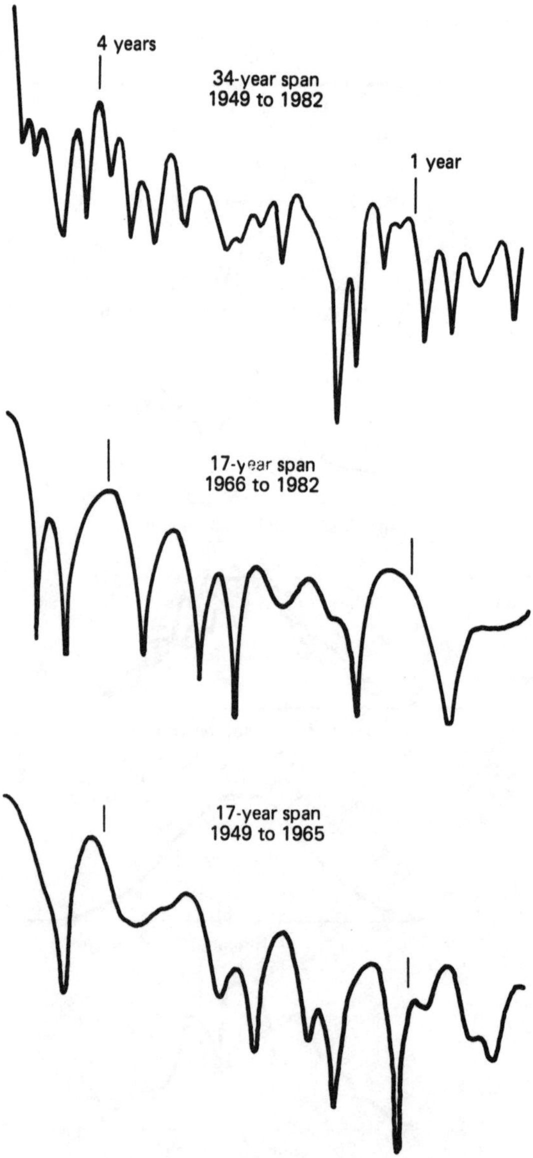

FIGURE 9-2. A longer span of data (top) produces finer resolution in the Fourier (frequency) plot (Dow Jones Industrials).

each generated by splitting the 34-year data series into two separate 17-year series, and each of these peaks is wider than the peak for the entire series at the top.

It also follows that when you find a peak broader than $1/T$ you can infer that the underlying oscillation was not of precisely constant amplitude and frequency throughout your data span.

The peak in Figure 9-1(b) also has another feature: "ears" on each side of the main "lobe". Some call these ears "side lobes". (Figure 5-3 shows a main lobe and side lobes for the moving average.) Mathematically, the cause is the same as for 9-1(b); the only difference is that 9-1(b) is two-sided because here we are modulating a frequency.

For comparison with 9-2, Figure 9-3 shows the (again, actual) frequency plots for two other, earlier periods of time. In this period the business cycle actually had a frequency that was somewhat higher than a 4-year period, as shown. In the bottom plot the frequency was higher still (3-year period); this was for 1933 to 1940, the years of stock price recovery after the crash of 1929.

Financial data are usually modulated by many factors, not just the duration of the data. If we were to take the Fourier transform of the construction industry data (Figure 8-1), we would doubtless obtain a plot resembling Figure 9-1(c). The top of the lobe would be at least $1/T$ wide but would be surrounded by its modulation products, and these would probably obscure the idealized side lobes shown in 9-1(b). (Figure 9-1(c) is not an actual Fourier transform; I do not have a data base for the construction industry.)

Figure 9-4 is the same real stock market data plotted on a broader scale to show any oscillations that may exist at higher frequencies than one cycle every three or four years.

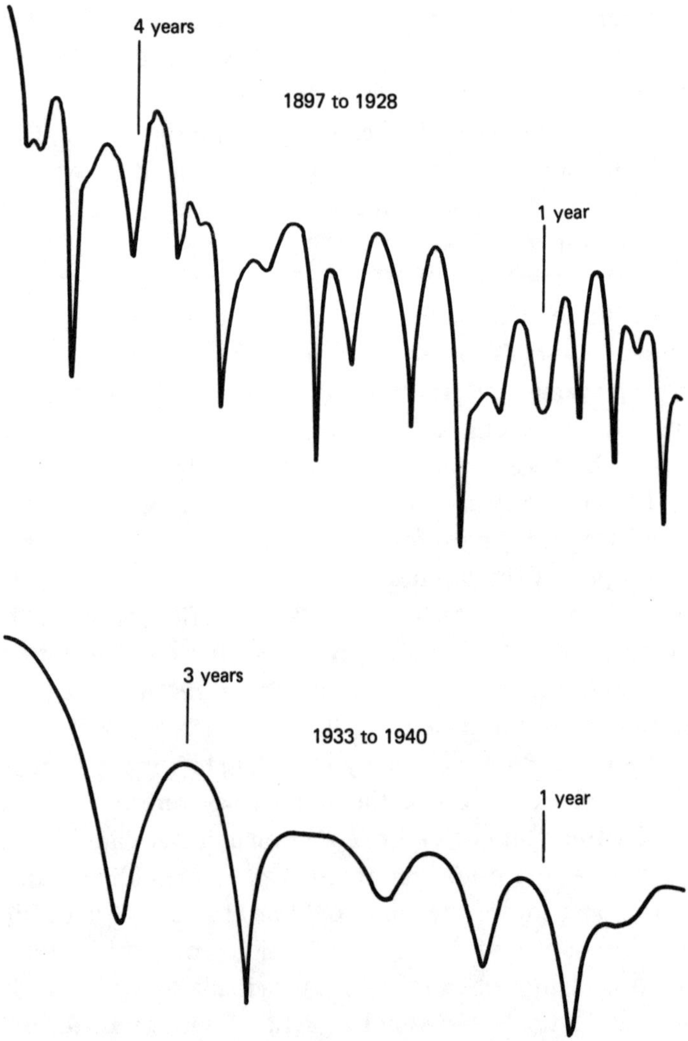

FIGURE 9-3. Frequency spectra for earlier periods of time (Dow Jones Industrials).

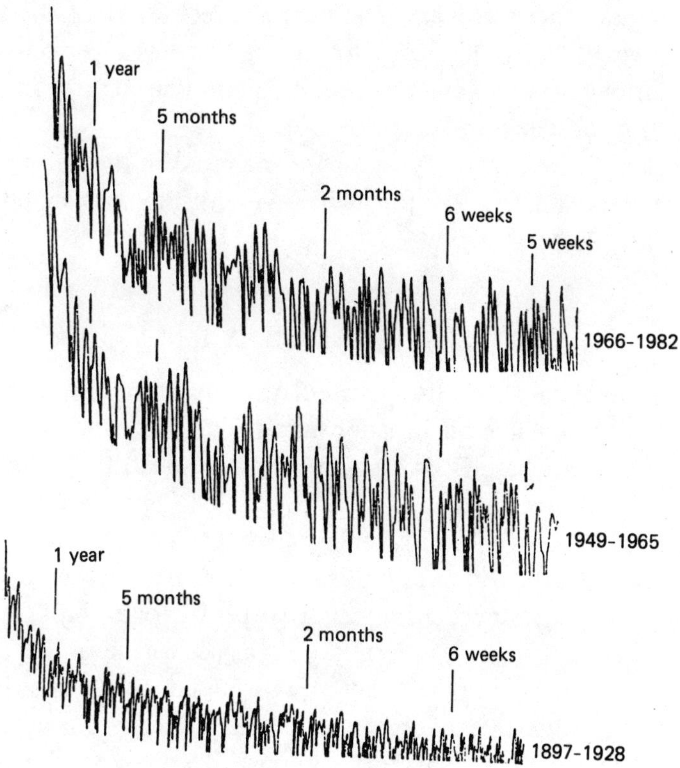

FIGURE 9-4. The higher frequencies in the Dow Jones Industrials. The lower trace was plotted on a different scale.

Again, the data were split up into segments to gain some idea of the persistence of any oscillation that might appear. The top trace shows an annual oscillation, but it is not prominent in the other traces; at least, not at precisely the same frequency. Also, a tendency toward oscillations appears to occur between two-and three-month periods in all three traces, but the frequency varies.

It is instructive to compare the peaks in the frequency spectra (Figures 9-2 through 9-4) with the corresponding time-plots in Chapter 7.

IRREGULAR OSCILLATIONS

We turn now to discuss oscillation peaks in the Fourier spectrum which are broader than $1/T$, T being the duration of the data base. This broadening of the spectrum peaks can tell us something about the oscillation. There are several possible causes for broadening, all quite different. Chapter 8 discussed the different kinds of oscillations, and we proceed now to examine the frequency spectrum for each of these.

First, I suggest a method you can use whenever you find a broad peak. I suggest that you divide your data series into shorter segments and recalculate the Fourier spectrum separately for each individual segment. If you carry this subdivision too far, eventually the spectrum peaks will become much wider than they were initially and there is no need to carry the segmentation that far.

Intermittent Oscillations

Suppose that the underlying source of the oscillation is as regular as clockwork but something modulates it before it affects the financial data, so that the oscillation comes through the process as *intermittent*. In this event, the width of the spectrum peak would be determined by the duration of the individual "pulses" or segments of the oscillation; and after we had segmented our data base and Fourier transformed the segments, we would expect to see strong spectrum peaks in some segments and weak peaks or none in others. In fact, if we desired to get a good look at the oscillation, we could move the segments around to maximize the spectral peak in some of them, and that should also maximize the oscillation in the data for that segment(s) and make the oscillation more visible in the (untransformed) data.

Now suppose you were to plot the spectrum of each of the individual data segments and plot them all on one paper so that they overlay each other. The result might look something like Figure 9-1(d).

Some people suspect that intermittent oscillations do exist. More than that, some suspect that oscillations *reverse* themselves from time to time. How can this happen? Here is one possible way. Suppose that so many businessmen bet on a regular cycle—such as the construction cycle—that the price of building materials was stabilized so much that the oscillation in their price was suppressed. Now suppose that suddenly one year the usual activity in construction was inhibited for some reason; in that case, the full warehouses could depress the price, and that would reverse the cycle for that season.

Such reversed cycles tend to reduce the height of the peak in a Fourier spectrum of the overall data base; segmentation of the data base prevents this and lets the peak show fully.

Resonance and Ringing

Next we consider intermittent oscillations which are *not* as regular as clockwork (the buzzword is "noncoherent"). They occur only when excited by some sudden event.

Figure 9–5 shows a single damped sinusoid, and its frequency spectrum is shown in Figure 9–1(e). If the data base contains several such sinusoids, then they can interfere with each other, producing a ragged frequency spectrum as in 9–1(f). (Actually, these spectra represent only the decaying sinusoid. The sudden onset of the oscillation also has its own spectrum, but it will be broad and probably not distinguishable from the other "noise".)

It is possible for a resonant (ringing) system to be excited again before its oscillation dies away. In that case it could oscillate continuously; but it would differ from an oscillation that had a precisely controlled frequency. The spectrum of the excited oscillation would be broader, and would look like Figure 9–1(f).

Sometimes the cause of damped oscillations can be identified by using the method of superimposed epochs.[1] A possible type of causative event is tested by using it to "line-up" the oscillations. If they then have the same phase so that they add up and reinforce each other, that type of event can be causally related to the oscillation.

Oscillations of Varying Frequency

Now suppose your oscillation was generated by an "on-off" action so that its amplitude might be fairly constant but its frequency changes from time to time. Your segmentation analysis might show that this is the case. The

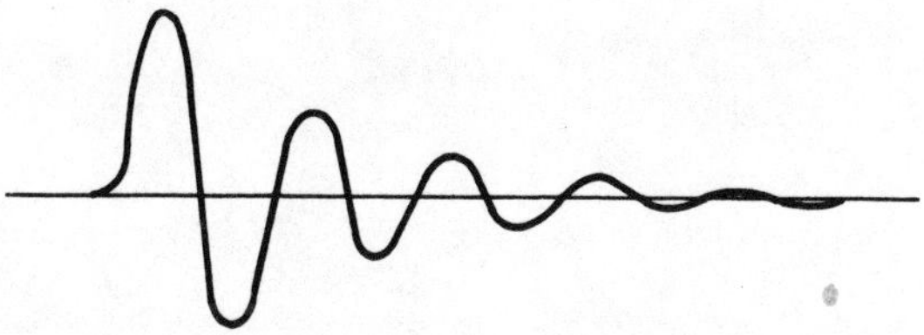

FIGURE 9-5. "Ringing" of a resonant system after a disturbance.

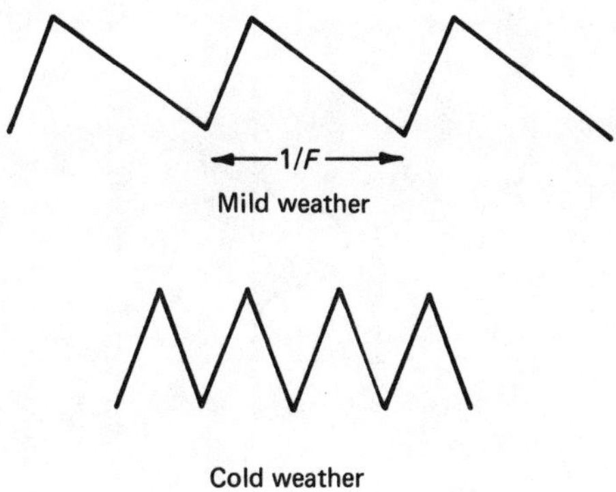

FIGURE 9-6. Variation of temperature with time with an on-off thermostat.

spectrum peak may appear in all your segments, but its frequency might vary from one segment to the next.

Of passing interest is another characteristic of the "triangular" oscillation of Figure 9–6 (Figure 8–2 repeated for further examination): It is rich in "harmonics," that is, additional spectral peaks at integral multiples (2x, 3x, etc.) of the fundamental frequency. These harmonics are shown in Figure 9–7, but they might not project above the "noise" in actual data because they are smaller than the peak at the fundamental frequency.

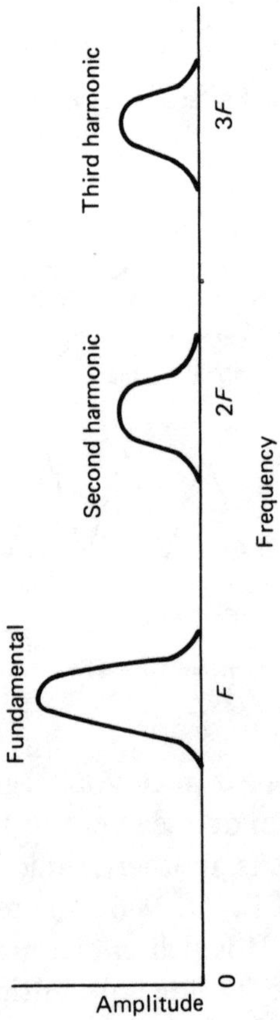

FIGURE 9-7. Spectrum of Figure 9-6, mild weather.

SUGGESTION FOR COMPUTER PROGRAMS

A researcher who does a lot of oscillation-hunting may eventually develop a set of standard programs for processing all kinds of data, and requiring little or no change to attack new data. At this point I suggest that the program generate several types of output from each "pass" of the data through the computer. If the program is a filter, it costs little more in computer time to include several different filters in the program. If it calculates the frequency spectrum, have it produce the spectrum not only for the complete time series, but also for each of several segments of the series. Filtering and spectrum calculation can be combined in a single program. These measures should save analysis time and reduce computer costs by reducing the total number of data passes required to reach a conclusion.

The Computer Program

The plots presented at the beginning of this chapter are relatively clear and free from noise. They did not start out that way. The magic touch finally arrived at (by trial-and-error) was a combination of de-trending and "windowing" (Figure 9–10).

De-trending

In the theory of the Fourier transform, each individual frequency arrayed in the spectrum is regarded as extending indefinitely forward and backward in time; that is, it is thought of as a continuous wave.

The time-series data can fit into such a pattern best only if it ends at the same value on which it began. If the beginning and the end are very different, the sudden jump will

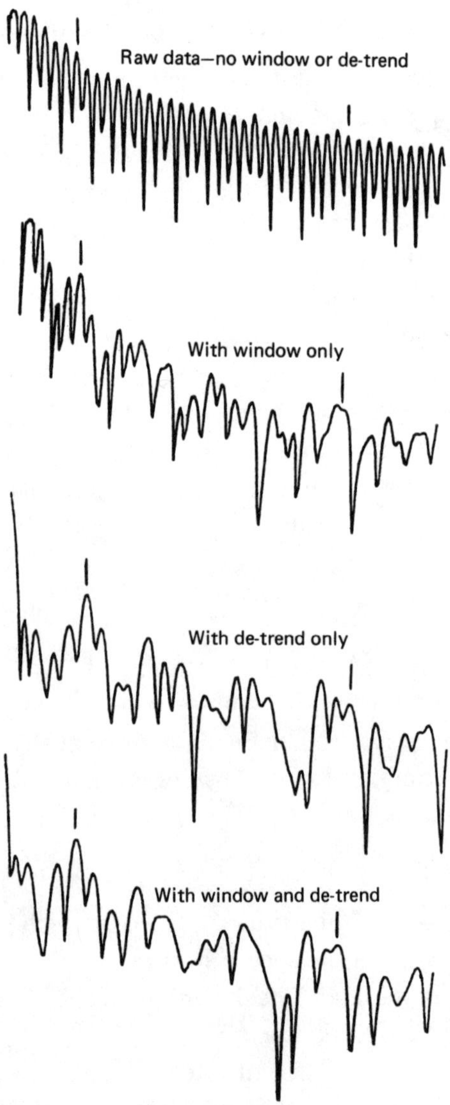

FIGURE 9-10. The frequency spectrum of untreated data (top) and the benefit of de-trending and windowing.

generate noise throughout the frequency spectrum and make it difficult to use.

Most real-world data are not so obliging; there is usually a trend upward or downward. What was done in this series was to de-trend it, that is, remove the trend. The slope between the first and last data points in the series was calculated (in the computer program), and this slope was subtracted from all the data points before they were processed by the Fourier transform.

Windowing

Windowing consists of "shaping" the data to reduce the splattering of noise over all frequencies. In Chapter 5, several different filter shapes were analyzed, and the preferred shapes were those having a low level of frequency sidebands. The principle of windowing is exactly the same, and the flat-topped shape of Figure 5-9, was used for the window. The entire data series was multiplied by the window values before being submitted to the Fourier transform routine. This can be seen in the program listing at the end of this chapter.

Program Description

The Fourier transform is of the FFT (Fast Fourier Transform) type, Cooley-Tukey algorithm. It is called by "CALL RHARM". It was used three times: First, on the de-trended data (for comparison); next, on the de-trended data after windowing; and finally, on a sine wave which was generated to "calibrate" the horizontal scale of the plot. The input data are at weekly intervals*, and the calibration sine wave has a period of one year.

---

*The input data are available in reference 2.

The output of the Fourier transform occurs in pairs of numbers, which must be combined; this was done by the SQRT routine after each application of RHARM. After the data were printed out, MEMSET was called to reset the A matrix to all-zeros. The rounded ends of the window were generated by DO-loops in the course of running the program.

The input data had previously been converted to logarithm form, and the output data were again converted to logarithms before plotting. The use of logarithms will be discussed in more detail in Chapter 10.

```
      PROGRAM H(INPUT=65, OUTPUT=65, PLOT,
     1  TAPE5=INPUT, TAPE6=OUTPUT, TAPE
     1  19=PLOT)
      DIMENSION X(1760), A(8200), INV(1025),
     1  S(1025)
      CALL MEMSTET(A(1), A(8200))
C
      N=880
C     LAST 880
C
      NH=N/2
C
      READ 25, (X(J), J=1,N)
   25 FORMAT (10F6.4)
C
C                   DE-TREND
C
      CN=N
      DELTA=(X(N)-X(1))/CN
      X1=X(1)
      DO 15 I=1, N
```

```
      X(I)=X(I)-X1-I*DELTA
       A(I)=X(I)
15    CONTINUE
      PRINT 35
35    FORMAT (1H1)
      PRINT 44, (X(J), J=1, N)
44    FORMAT (1H, 5F 9.4, 1H, 5F 9.4)
C
20    CALL RHARM (A, 12, INV, S, IFERR)
      J=1
      DO 16 I=1, NH
      J1=J+1
      A(I)=SQRT(AJ)**2+A(J1)**2)
      J=J+2
16    CONTINUE
      PRINT 35
      PRINT 46, (A(J), J=1, NH)
46    FORMAT(1H, 5F10.6, 4X, 5F10.6)
      CALL MEMSET (A(1), A(8200))
C
C                 WINDOW
C
      N1=N/4-100
      AN1=N1
      DO 80 I=1, N1
      AI=I
      ANGLE=90*AI/AN1
      A(I)=X(I)*SIND(ANGLE)
80    CONTINUE
      N1=N1+1
      N3=100+3*N/4
      DO 82 I=NI, N3
      A(I)=X(I)
82    CONTINUE
      N3=N3+1
```

```
      AN=N
      DO 85 I=N3, N
      AI=I
      ANGLE=360*(1-AI/AN)
      A(I)=X(I)*SIND(ANGLE)
85    CONTINUE
      PRINT 35
      PRINT 44, (A(J), J=1, N)
      CALL HARM (A, 12, INV, S, IFERR)
      J=1
      DO 17 I=1, NH
      J1=J+1
      A(I)=SQRT(A(J)**2+A(J1)**2)
        A(I)=ALOG10(A(I))
      J=J+2
17    CONTINUE
      PRINT 35
      PRINT 46, (A(J), J=1, NH)
C
C                          PLOT
C
      CALL PLOTSQ(0, 0, 19)
      CALL OBJEG(.8, 1.2, 6.0, 2.5)
      CALL PAGE
      CALL SUBJEG(0, -4.0, 440., 1.2)
      CALL LINEG1(440, A, 1., 1.)
      CALL EXITG
C
      CALL MEMSET (A(1), A(8200))
C
C     SINE WAVE FOR FREQUENCY CHECK
C
      DO 13 I=I, 8200
      AI=I
      ANGLE=360*(AI/52.18)
```

```
 90          A(I)=SIND(ANGLE)
        13   CONTINUE
             CALL HARM (A, 12, INV, S, IFERR)
        C
             J=1
 95          DO 18 I=1, NH
             J1=J+1
             A(I)=SQRT(A(J)**2+A(J1)**2)
             J=J+2
        18   CONTINUE
100          PRINT 35
             PRINT 46, (A(J), J=1, NH)
             STOP
             END
```

REFERENCES

1. Craddock, J.M. *Statistics in the Computer Age.* American Elsevier. 1969.
2. Dow Jones Irwin, The Dow Jones Averages, 1885-1980.

APPENDIX TO CHAPTER NINE

Duality of Spectral and Time Response

The frequency spectrum is mathematically and completely determined by the shape of the fluctuation versus time. The Fourier transform connects the two shapes.

In "Effect of Data Duration" in this chapter we saw that a spectral peak much broader than that of a pure sine wave shows that the amplitude and/or the frequency of the oscillation must be varying. You can also say that the spectrum contains more than one sine wave component. The two statements say the same thing—one with reference to a time plot, the other with reference to a frequency plot. The "in" buzzwords are *time domain* and *frequency domain.* Sometimes one viewpoint is simpler (therefore better), sometimes the other.

The Spectrum of Resonant Ringing

The width of the spectrum is related to how rapidly the oscillation decays. A broad spectrum goes with rapid decay. The fractional bandwidth (between half-power–.7 amplitude–frequencies) equals the (natural, or base *e*) logarithmic decrement from one cycle to the next (Figure 9-8) divided by pi:

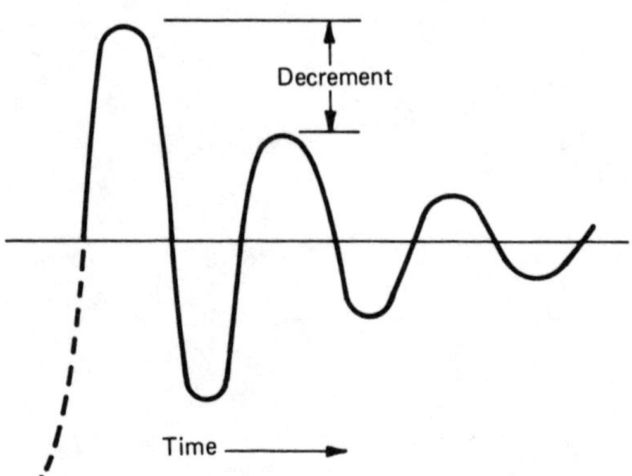

FIGURE 9-8. Resonant ringing.

$$\frac{\Delta f}{f_o} = \log_e (\text{decrement}) \div \pi \qquad \text{(Reference 1)}$$

Figure 9-8 shows ringing with each cycle decayed to one-half the amplitude of the previous cycle. The decrement in this example is Log_e (½), which is .69 (dropping the algebraic sign), so the bandwidth is:

$$\frac{\Delta f}{f_o} = .69 \div \pi = 22\% \qquad \text{(Figure 9-9)}$$

If the decay is less abrupt so that the ringing is more sustained, the relationship approaches simply:

$$(\%\ \text{bandwidth}) = (\%\ \text{decrement}) \div \pi$$

The above spectrum is for the decaying oscillation only and does not include the beginning of the waveform shown in Figure 9-8. Inasmuch as the start-up is usually abrupt, its spectrum is broad, of low amplitude, and indistinguishable from the background "noise" of the data.

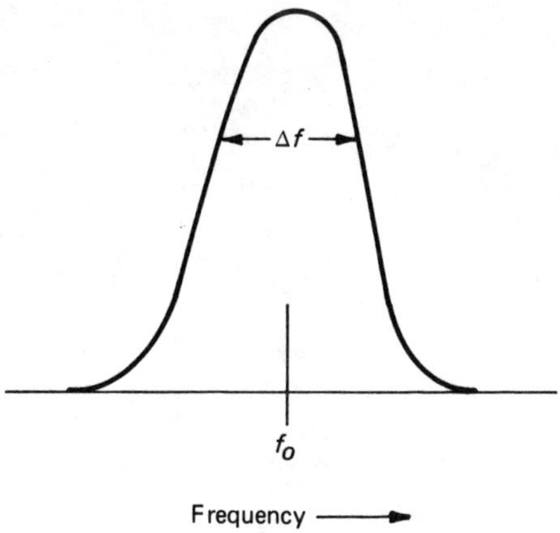

FIGURE 9-9. Spectrum of resonant ringing.

REFERENCE TO APPENDIX

1. Guillemin, E.A., *Introductory Circuit Theory*. Wiley. 1953.

10
Nonlinearity and Aliasing

All that glitters is not gold.
ARISTOTLE

NONLINEARITY

Options have a nonlinear response as shown in Figure 10–1. An option to buy ("call option" or "warrant") is a contract which permits the holder to purchase shares of stock at a certain specified price. This is called "exercising" the option. If the price of the stock rises, then by exercising the option the holder can make a profit; if the price of the stock falls then he would not exercise the option but would let it expire. This is shown by the solid line in 10–1.

The break in the solid line is what I am calling the nonlinearity. One of its attractions is "downside protection". By this I mean that the price of the underlying stock can drop as low as it wishes and this will not concern the holder of the option–he acts only on the "up" side. Of course, he would be foolish to risk *all* his money in options because the downside "protection" could clean him out.

Theoretically, a gambler can make money by using this downside protection on volatile stocks. (A communication engineer would say he was using a rectifier to get some en-

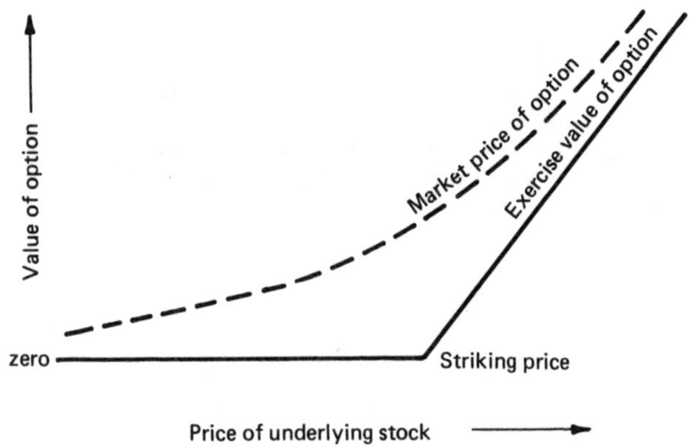

FIGURE 10-1. The value of an option is nonlinear.

ergy out of noise.) This is a well-recognized possibility, and for that reason the buyer of an option pays a premium above the exercise value of the option; the dashed line in Figure 10–1 shows the resulting market price.

Buying options is a mistake for most people–I write that from personal experience. My main reason for bringing them up at all is intellectual–they are excellent examples of nonlinearity.

Interestingly, low-priced stocks also tend to react like the dashed line in 10–1, and for this reason I almost never "sell short". Selling short is selling stock that you do not own in the hope that you can buy it in later at a cheaper price and thus make a profit. The trouble with selling short a nonlinear stock or option is that you do not stand to gain much on the downside, but you could really lose your shirt on the upside.

Effect of Nonlinearity on the Frequency Spectrum

Nonlinearity can cause *distortion* and *intermodulation* of the data. Distortion is a deformation of the wave shape which produces "harmonics" of any oscillations present (Figure 10–2); these harmonics occur at integral multiples (2x, 3x, etc.) of the frequency of the fundamental (main) oscillation. The degree of the distortion, and hence the amplitude of the harmonics, relative to that of the fundamental is proportional (more or less) to the amplitude of the fundamental; if that is small, the harmonics will be much smaller still.

Intermodulation is an interaction between fluctuations to produce sum and difference frequencies. The amplitudes of the sum and difference frequencies are proportional (more or less) to the amplitudes of *each* of the intermodulating fluctuations.

These effects are noticeable only when the nonlinearity is great, and it sometimes is. For example, it is natural to

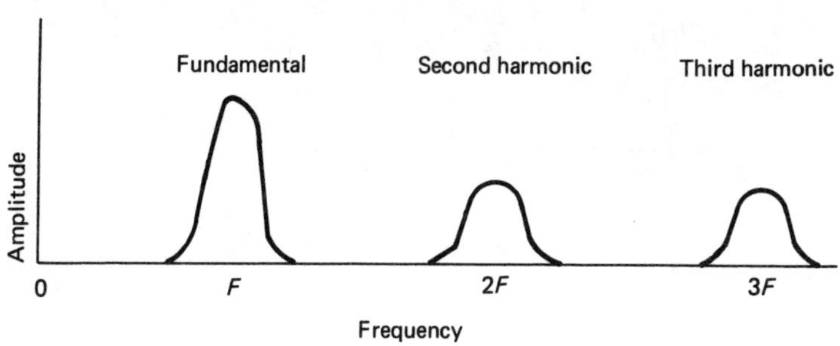

FIGURE 10-2. Harmonics generated in the frequency spectrum of an oscillation by nonlinearity.

measure *visibility* in terms of distance (miles). But smoke affects the *turbidity* of the air, and visibility is an *inverse function* of turbidity. The data vary widely, two orders of magnitude or more, so visibility is a highly nonlinear function of the amount of smoke in the air (Figure 10-3). For someone analyzing this time series, turbidity might give simpler (hence better) results than visibility.

Filtering Logarithms

The stock price index data summarized in Chapter 7 were converted to logarithms before filtering. This was done because of the wide range of the data—from 30 to 1,000. In Figure 7-2 it made little difference whether the data or its logarithms were filtered because the deviation of the data within the span of the filter was usually less than ±10%, and

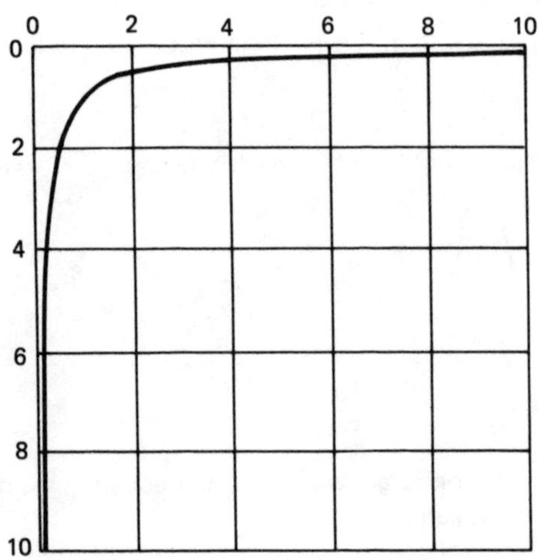

FIGURE 10-3. The inverse function is strongly nonlinear when covering a 100:1 range.

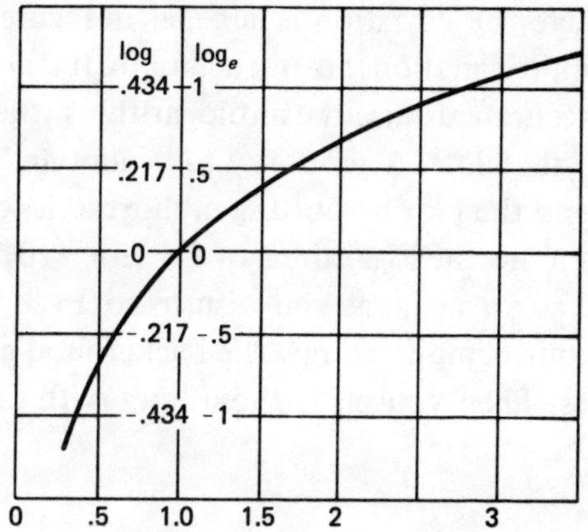

FIGURE 10-4. Nonlinearity of logarithm function over 10:1 range.

always less than ±20%. Figure 10–4 shows that the logarithm is a sufficiently linear function of the number over this range for the difference to be ignored.

However, if the deviation within the filter span were greater, say +100%, −50% or more, you must decide whether it is better to smooth the data or its logarithms. In this particular time series, I would still prefer to smooth the logarithms, though I am not sure how strongly I can justify that preference.

When smoothing logarithms, the output of the filters is of course logarithmic also. Where the deviation is small, it is simple to apply an approximate scale by using one of the following rules:

1. When using natural (base *e*) logarithms, percent deviation is 100x (times) the data deviation.
2. When using common (base 10) logarithms, percent deviation is 230.26x the data deviation.

But where the deviation is large, as in Figure 7–4, then the above approximations are not accurate. It is always valid, and more accurate, to use the antilogarithms when marking the scale of the plots. A good way to "calibrate" a plot is to begin and end the plot by putting in short series of constant values which are the logarithms of 1.1 (for +10%), 0.9 (for -10%), and so on, as far as you wish to go. Even better, you can have your computer draw the background grid lines at these values. Then you mark these lines with the antilogarithm (+10%, etc.)

AVOIDING ALIASING

The price of a security is quoted for a particular time, such as the closing of the market. This is called *sampling* of the data. Sampling is a very nonlinear process, but we cannot easily avoid it, so it is important to understand its effects and avoid being deceived by them. One of these bad effects is *aliasing**.

Aliasing is a process by which a high frequency oscillation is repeated (duplicated) at a lower frequency. A low frequency oscillation caused by aliasing is of course spurious, so we need to recognize it and to avoid treating it as a real oscillation in the data.

Aliasing results from modulation of the data by the sampling frequency and its harmonics, so it appears at their sum and difference frequencies, as shown in Figure 10–5(a). But only the lowest of these difference frequencies is of interest, because we always ignore the spectrum above one-

*Communications engineers call it "heterodyning".

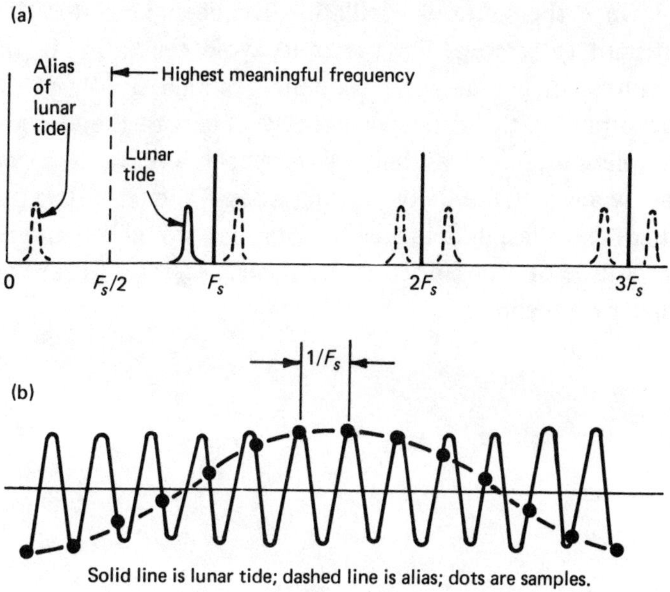

FIGURE 10-5. Explanation of aliasing (top) and resulting spectrum (bottom), *Fs* is the sampling frequency.

half the sampling frequency. It merely consists of the lower spectrum folded back and then repeated indefinitely.

As an example of aliasing, suppose you measured the water level in a tidal basin twice each day, say at 12 o'clock. The period of the lunar tide is just under 13 hours, so it gradually gets "out of step" and then "in step" with your measurements–their relative phase varies, as shown in Figure 10-5(b). As a result, your data will contain a strong oscillation which appears to have a period of about 15 days (the difference between the lunar tide frequency and the sampling frequency). But the water level does not contain a 15-day oscillation: what you are looking at is the lunar tide converted to a lower frequency by aliasing.

Once the spurious oscillation has been generated, it is difficult to remove. Far better to avoid generating it; this requires a higher sampling frequency. In Figures 7–1 and 7–2, the input to the filter was weekly data, but the effective sampling interval was daily because each weekly figure was the average of the daily closing index. Daily sampling produces less aliasing than weekly sampling would because the amplitude of stock price fluctuations decreases toward the higher frequencies.

FURTHER READING

Chapter 2

Appel, Gerald, and Hitschler, W. Frederick, *Stock Market Trading Systems,* Dow Jones-Irwin, 1980.

Cobleigh, Ira U., *Happiness is a Stock that Doubles in a Year,* Signet, 1977.

Newman, Joseph, *How to Find a Growth Stock,* U. S. News (book), 1973.

Chapter 3

Walpole, Ronald E., and Myers, Raymond H., *Probability and Statistics for Engineers and Scientists,* Macmillan, 1972.

Chapter 5

Priestley, M.B., *Spectral Analysis and Time Series,* vol. 1, Academic Press, 1981.

Rabiner, L.R. "The Design of Finite Impulse Response Digital Filters Using Linear Programming Techniques," *Bell Systems Technical Journal.*, July-Aug. 1972.

Chapter 6

Antoniou, A., *Digital Filters: Analysis and Design,* McGraw-Hill, 1979.

Blackman, R.B. *Data Smoothing and Prediction,* Addison-Wesley, 1965.

Bogner, R.E., and Constantinides, A.G., *Introduction to Digital Filtering,* Wiley Interscience, 1975.

Box, G.E.P., and Jenkins, G.M. *Time Series Analysis, Forecasting and Control.* Holden-Day, 1970.

Brown, R.G. *Smoothing, Forecasting and Prediction of Discrete Time Series.* Prentice-Hall, 1962.

Bruce, J.D., "Discrete Fourier Transforms, Linear Filters and Spetrum Weighting," *IEEE Transactions on Audio and Electroacoustics,* Vol. AU-16, No. 4 (Dec. 1968). pp. 494–499.

Cootner, P. *The Random Character of Stock Market Prices.* MIT Press, 1964.

Daniels, Richard W. *Approximation Methods for Electronic Filter Design,* McGraw-Hill, 1974.

Davenport, W.B., Jr. *Probability and Random Processes.* McGraw-Hill, 1970.

Fishman, G.S. *Spectral Methods in Economics.* Harvard University Press, 1969.

Fung. A.K., "On Numerical Evaluation of Power Density Spectra of Random Functions." *IEEE Transactions on Audio and Electroacoustics* (Dec. 1968), pp. 527–528.

Gold, B., and Rader, C.M. *Digital Processing of Signals.* McGraw-Hill, 1969.

Golden, Roger M., "Digital Filters," Chapter 12 in Temes & Mitra, *Modern Filter Theory and Design,* Wiley-Interscience, 1973.

Hamming, R.W. *Numerical Methods for Scientists and Engineers,* McGraw-Hill, 1973.

Harmuth, H.F. *A Generalized Concept of Frequency and Some Applications.* IEEE Transactional Information Theory, May 1968.

Harris, Frederic J., "On the use of Windows for Harmonic Analysis with the Discrete Fourier Transform," *Proc. IEEE,* January 1978.

Kaiser, J.F., "Digital Filters," part of *Kuo and Kaiser, System Analysis by Digital Computer,* Wiley, 1966.

Kuo, B.C. *Digital Control Systems,* SRL (Champaign, IL), 1977.

Lindorff, D.P. *Theory of Sampled-Data Control Systems,* Wiley, 1965.

Lubkin, Y.J. *Filter Systems and Design.,* Addison-Wesley, 1970.

Lynn, Paul A. *An Introduction to the Analysis and Processing of Signals,* Wiley, 1973.

Morrison, N. *Introduction to Sequential Smoothing and Prediction.* McGraw-Hill, 1969.

Negron, C.D., "Digital One-Third Octave Spectral Analysis," *Jour. Assoc. for Comp. Machinery,* Vol. 13, No. 4 (Oct. 1966), pp. 605-614.

Oppenheim, A.V. *Papers on Digital Signal Processing.* MIT Press, 1969.

Otnes, Robert K., and Enochson, Loren. *Applied Time Series Analysis,* Wiley, 1978.

Rabiner, et al, "Terminology in Digital Signal Processing," *IEEE Transactions on Audio & Electroacoustics,* Dec 1972.

Rabiner, L.A., and Rader, C.M., *Digital Signal Processing,* IEEE Press, 1972.

Rader, C.M., and B. Gold, "Digital Filter Design Techniques in the Frequency Domain," *Proc. IEEE,* Vol. 55, No. 2 (Feb. 1967), pp. 149-171.

Ragazzini, J.R., and Franklin, G.F. *Sampled-Data Control Systems,* McGraw, 1958.

Robinson, E.A., and Silvia, M.T. *Digital Signal Processing and Time Series Analysis,* Holden-Day, 1978.

Robinson, E.A., and S. Treitel, "Principles of Digital Filtering," *Geophysics,* Vol. XXIX, No. 3 (June 1964), pp. 395-404.

Salzman, L. *Computerized Economic Analysis.* McGraw-Hill, 1968.

Schwartz, L.S. *Principles of Coding, Filtering and Information Theory.* Spartan, 1963.

Shaw, H., "Discrete Analogs for Continuous Filters," *Jour. Assoc. for Comp. Machinery,* Vol. 13, No. 4 (Oct. 1966), pp. 600-604.

Shreve, James S., "Digital Signal Processing," chapter 35 of Skolnik, *Radar Handbook,* McGraw-Hill, 1970.

Shubik, M. *Essays in Mathematical Economics.* Princeton University Press, 1967.

Stanley, W.D. *Digital Signal Processing,* Reston, 1975.

Stuart, R.D. *An Introduction to Fourier Analysis.* Methuen, 1961.

Taylor, Fred and Smith, Steve L. *Digital Signal Processing in Fortran,* Lexington Books, 1976.

Tou, J.T., *Digital and Sampled-Data Control Systems,* McGraw-Hill, 1959.

Truxal, J.G., *Automatic Feedback Control System Synthesis,* McGraw-Hill, 1955.

Wiener, N. *The Fourier Integral and Certain of its Applications.* Dover, 1958 (orig. 1933).

Woodside, C.M., "The Interpretation of Time-Domain Models in the Frequency Domain," *IEEE Transactions on Automatic Control,* (Feb. 1967), pp. 110–111.

Yeatman, W.C., "A Method for Separating Cycles and its Use in Conjunction with Other Methods," *Jour. Cycle Research,* Vol. 4, No. 4 (Oct. 1955).

Chapter 7

American Institute for Economic Research Bulletins: Harwood, E.C., "Cause and Control of the Business Cycle," 1974; Harwood, E.C., "Reconstruction of Economics," 1970; Sparks, Richard P., "Forecasting Business Trends," 1978.

Burns, Arthur F., *The Business Cycle in a Changing World,* Columbia University Press, 1969.

Cootner, P. *The Random Character of Stock Market Prices,* MIT Press, 1964.

Hayes, Michael, "The Dow Jones-Irwin Guide to Stock Market Cycles," Dow Jones-Irwin, 1977.

Klein, Roger, and Wolman, William. *The Beat Inflation Strategy,* Simon and Schuster, 1975.

No-Load Mutual Fund Association, Valley Forge, PA, 19481.

Tufte, Edward R., *Political Control of the Economy,* Princeton University Press, 1978.

Woytinsky, W.S. and E.S., "Lessons of the Recessions," Public Affairs Institute, 1959.

Chapter 8

Anderson, James E. *Politics and the Economy,* Little.

Burns, Arthur F. *The Business Cycle in a Changing World,* Columbia University Press, 1969.

Estey, James Arthur. *Business Cycles: Their Nature, Cause and Control,* Prentice-Hall, 1956.

Tufte, Edward R., *Political Control of the Economy,* Princeton University Press, 1978.

Chapter 9

Armstrong, C.E., "Testing Cycles for Statistical Significance," *Jour. Cycle Research* (Spring 1952).

Barber, N.F. *Experimental Correlograms and Fourier Transforms.* Pergamon Press, 1961.

Bloomfield, Peter. *Fourier Analysis of Time Series: An Introduction,* Wiley, 1976.

Box, G.E.P., and Jenkins, G.M.. *Time Series Analysis, Forecasting and Control,* Holden-Day, 1970.

Granger, C.W.J., and M. Hatanaka. *Spectral Analysis of Economic Time Series;* Princeton University Press, 1964 ed.

Hannan, E.J. *Time Series Analysis,* Science Paperbacks (Methuen), 1960.

Harris, Bernard. *Introduction to the Theory of Spectral Analysis of Time Series,* part of *Spectral Analysis of Time Series,* Wiley, 1967.

I.T. & T. *Reference Data for Radio Engineers.* Howard W. Sams & Co., 1968.

Lange, F.H. *Correlation Techniques.* Iliffe (London), D. Van Nostrand, 1967.

Lynn, Paul A.. *An Introduction to the Analysis and Processing of Signals,* Wiley, 1973.

Mason, S.J., and Zimmermann., H.J. *Electronic Circuits, Signals and Systems.* Wiley, 1960 ed.

Maurice, R.D.A.. *Convolution and Fourier Transforms for Communications Engineers,* Pentech Press (London), 1976.

Stuart, R.D. *An Introduction to Fourier Analysis,* Science Paperbacks (Methuen), 1961.

GENERAL

There are many available books on investment. Read as many as you can and *always* take any investment advice with a grain of salt. None of it is guaranteed to produce a profit.

PERSONAL MONEY MANAGEMENT

Hallman, G. Victor, and Rosenbloom, Jerry S., *Personal Financial Planning.*

Porter, Sylvia, *Sylvia Porter's New Money Book for the 80's.*

Quinn, Jane Bryant, *Everyone's Money Book.*

Van Caspel, Venita, *Money Dynamics for the 1980s.*

GENERAL INVESTMENT INFORMATION

Christy, George A., and Clendenin, John C., *Introduction to Investments.*

Crane, Burton, *The Sophisticated Investor,* Simon & Schuster, 1964.

Dow Jones Investor's Handbook (annual), Princeton, NJ.

Dow Jones-Irwin Books, 1818 Ridge Road, Homewood, IL 60430. Send for catalog.

Graham, Benjamin, *The Intelligent Investor,* Harper, 1949.

Graham, Benjamin, et al, *Security Analysis.*

Harper, Victor L., *Handbook of Investment, Products and Services.*

Malkiel, Burton, *The Inflation-Beater's Investment Guide,* W.W. Norton, 1980. Excellent.

Mayer, Martin, *Wall Street Men and Money,* Collier (Macmillan), 1955.

Rukeyser, Louis, How to Make Money in Wall Street, Doubleday, 1974.

Sarnoff, P., *Wall Street Wisdom,* Pocket Books, 1965. Formerly called *The Wall Street Thesaurus.*

Sokolof, Kiril, *The Thinking Investor's Guide to the Stock Market.*

Tracy, John A., *How to Read a Financial Report.*

United Business Service Staff, *Successful Investing, A Complete Guide to Your Financial Future,* Simon & Schuster, 1979. An excellent reference book.

BONDS

Darst, David, *The Complete Bond Book.*

Darst, David, *The Handbook of the Bond and Money Markets.*

CAUTIONARY

Barmash, Isadore, *Great Business Disasters,* Ballantine, 1972.

Baruch, M., *Wall Street: Security Risk,* Penguin, 1971.

Brutus, *Confessions of a Stockbroker,* Little, Brown, 1971.

Darvas, N., *Wall Street, the Other Las Vegas,* Ace, 1964.

Dirks, Raymond L., And Gross, Leonard, *The Great Wall Street Scandal–Inside Equity Funding,* McGraw-Hill, 1974.

Elias, C., *Fleecing the Lambs,* H. Regnery Co.

Goldston, Robert, *The Great Depression,* Fawcett, 1968.

Hazard, C.C., *Confessions of a Wall Street Insider,* Playboy Press, 1972.

Mackay, C., *Extraordinary Popular Delusions and the Madness of Crowds,* 1841; reprinted 1962 by L.C. Page & Co.

Malkiel, Burton G., *A Random Walk Down Wall Street,* W.W. Norton, 1973.

Manne, Henry G., *Insider Trading and the Stock Market,* Free Press (Macmillan) 1966.

Patterson, Robert T., *The Great Boom and Panic.*

Tobias, Andrew, *The Funny Money Game,* Playboy Press, 1971.

Tobias, Andrew, *Getting By on $100,000 a Year and Other Sad Tales,* Simon & Schuster, 1980.

Tobias, Andrew, *The Only Investment Guide You'll Ever Need,* Harcourt Brace Jovanovich, 1978.

Train, John, *Dance of the Money Bees–A Professional Speaks Frankly on Investing,* Harper & Row, 1974.

CHARTING

Edwards and Magee, *Technical Analysis of Stock Trends,* Magee, 1962.

Jiler, W., *How Charts Can Help You in the Stock Market.*

REAL ESTATE

Antony Schools, *The Real Estate Handbook,* Newport Beach, CA.

Cooley, Leland F. and Lee M., *The Simple Truth About Western Land Investment,* Doubleday, 1968.

Creedy, Judith, and Wall, Norbert, *Real Estate Investment by Objective.*

English, John Wesley, and Cardiff, Gray Emerson, *The Coming Real Estate Crash,* Warner Books, 1979.

Harrison, Henry S. and Leonard, Margery B., *Home Buying,* Realtors National Marketing Institute.

Kirk, John E., *How to Build a Fortune Investing in Land,* Prentice-Hall, 1973.

Koch, James H., *Profits from Country Property.*

Pratt, Lawrence S., *Home Owner or Tenant? How to Make a Wise Choice,* American Institute for Economic Research, 1977.

Winnikoff, Albert, *The Land Game, or How to Make a Fortune in Real Estate,* Lyle Stuart, 1970.

WIDOWHOOD

Kirsch, Charlotte, *A Survivor's Manual.*

Newman, Joseph, *Teach Your Wife to be a Widow.*

MISCELLANEOUS

Berton, Lee, "Investing by Computer: Can you Beat the Market?", *Financial World,* July 17, 1974.

"Why Some Experts Say You Can't Beat the Stock Averages," *Changing Times,* May 1980.

Chicago Mercantile Exchange, Bibliography and Information Source List (free).

Emory, Eric S., *When to Sell Stocks–Portfolio Liquidation: the Key to Superior Performance Without Stock Selection,* Dow Jones-Irwin, 1973.

"Discount Brokers: Don't Discount Them," *Financial World,* February 7, 1973.

Freeman, W.H., "A Comprehensive Review of the Extraordinary New Technology of Information", Scientific American, 1966.

Galbraith, John Kenneth, "The Great Wall Street Crash," *The New Republic,* 1979.

Goldston, Robert, *The Great Depression,* Fawcett, 1968.

Grant, Neil, *The Industrial Revolution,* Franklin Watts, Inc., 1973.

Greenfield, Samuel C., *The Low-High Theory of Investment, How to Make Money in the Stock Market–and Keep It,* Coward-McCann, Inc., 1968.

Gunther, Max, *The Very, Very Rich and How They Got That Way,* Playboy Press, 1972.

Hoppe, *How to Invest in Gold Stocks . . .*

Klein, Frederick C., and Prestbo, John A., *News and the Market,* Henry Regnery, 1974.

Markstein, David L., *Nine Roads to Wealth.*

Miller, Jarrott T., *The Long and the Short of Hedging,* Henry Regnery, 1973.

Moscato, Donald R., *Building Financial Decision-Making Models,* Amacom, 1980.

Noddings, Thomas C., *How the Experts Beat the Market, The Strategy and Tactics for Greatly Increasing the Odds in Your Favor,* Dow Jones-Irwin, 1976.

Rosenberg, C., *Psycho-Cybernetics and the Stock Market,* Playboy Press, 1971.

Sarnoff, Paul, *Jesse Livermore: Speculator-King,* Investors' Press, 1967.

Schultz, Harry, *Panics and Crashes and How You Can Make Money Out of Them,* Pinnacle, 1972.

Sinclair, James E., and Schultz, Harry D., *How the Experts Buy and Sell Gold Bullion, Gold Stocks and Gold Coins,* Arlington House, 1975.

Sobel, Robert, *The Worldly Economists,* The Free Press (Macmillan).

Thomas, Dana, *The Money Crowd,* Warner, 1973.

Vicker, Ray, *Those Swiss Money Men,* Chas. Scribner's.

Walton, Sidney, "Secrets of Speculation", Profit Re$earch, 1958.

INDEX

P

R

S

T

U

V

W

X

Z